Tony

GWYNN'S

TOTAL
BASEBALL
PLAYER

Tony GWYNN'S

TOTAL BASEBALL PLAYER

Tony Gwynn

with
Jim Rosenthal

Photos by
Russ Gilbert

ST. MARTIN'S PRESS
NEW YORK

Design and layout by Judith A. Stagnitto

Library of Congress Cataloging-in-Publication Data

Gwynn, Tony.
        [Total baseball player]
        Tony Gwynn's total baseball player / Tony
Gwynn with Jim Rosenthal.
                p.   cm.
        ISBN 0-312-07097-7. —ISBN 0-312-07098-5
(pbk.)
        1. Baseball.   I. Rosenthal, Jim.   II. Title.
    GV867.G98   1992   796.357—dc20   91-41820

First Edition: April 1992
10 9 8 7 6 5 4 3 2 1

CONTENTS

FOREWORD

Willie Davis

Tony Gwynn is a quiet leader, a guy who does his job without complaining, works hard—day in and day out, and encourages and motivates other players simply by showing them the right way to do things.

Tony leads by example. He's a great contact hitter, a Gold Glove outfielder and a talented baserunner. But there's more to it than that: He's always on time. He gets to the ballpark early to take extra batting practice. Tony is, in fact, the first player to arrive at the park every single day. The guys on the team know he can be relied on; he'll give his all every game to help the club win.

Tony and I have a lot in common: the simple, effortless style of play; a no-nonsense approach; a love for the game. I'm honored that he used to come out to Dodger Stadium when he was a kid just to watch me play center field. Like Tony, I believe in leading by example—setting a positive tone for

the team, being consistent and striving to win.

You have to cultivate a winning attitude from the very first day you grab a bat and ball. It begins with the fundamentals—backing up in the outfield, hitting the cut-off man, the little things that win games.

I signed with the Dodgers out of Roosevelt High School in Los Angeles in 1958. Ron Meyers, the scout who discovered me, stressed focusing on the basics. He knew I could run like the wind; it was just a matter of learning the tools of the trade.

Ron believed in me. His confidence in my ability reinforced my desire to succeed. We spent six months together, going over every possible situation and skill. And the hard work paid off—I made the Dodger ball club after only two minor league seasons.

Those Dodger teams of the 1960s had a winning tradition, a winning spirit.

We'd gather together before a game and talk about winning; we were proud to be Dodgers. Sandy Koufax would say, "Just get me two runs; that's all I need."

Winning eliminates the negative energy and distractions that tend to mess up your mind. Frankly, I think many people take baseball too seriously. Learn to have fun. Come to the park or playground with the idea you're going to enjoy yourself—regardless of how you perform that day. I enjoyed every game I ever played. Just do your best and work hard for your rewards.

That's what Tony does. He emphasizes doing the little things to help his team win games. He's proud to make his living playing baseball. And he is a quality person, a guy who literally personifies the San Diego Padres. The people of San Diego love Tony, and that's because he's given them years of pleasure just by being true to himself.

You can't be a successful baseball player unless you're a decent human being. I tell people that and they wonder, but I know in my heart that it's true. If you're really a good guy, then special things will happen to you. The good luck will fall your way—you'll win games and capture championships.

Strive to be a giving person, a trusted teammate and a caring friend. Follow the right path and you'll discover that everything will work out for you in baseball. And the first step on the right path is to listen to Tony Gwynn, the genuine "Total Baseball Player" of his generation.

ACKNOWLEDGMENTS

Tony Gwynn

I'd like to thank my wife, Alicia, who has been at my side through thick and thin, the good times and the bad, for her love and support. My children, Anisha and Tony Jr. The San Diego Padres for giving me an opportunity. My parents, Charles and Vendella Gwynn, for putting me here on this earth and teaching me values I've been able to use on the baseball field. My agent, John Boggs, for the chance to write this book. And last but not least, the good Lord above who has blessed me with the ability to do the things I've been able to do.

Jim Rosenthal

To my wife and family for their continued support. Special thanks to John Boggs, Shari Wenk, and George Witte for their invaluable assistance. And to Tony Gwynn, a great player and an equally great individual.

Tony

GWYNN'S

TOTAL BASEBALL PLAYER

INTRODUCTION

I'M always looking to find an edge, something that's going to make me the best player I can be. I can't just go out and play on ability. If I play on ability I won't be in the big leagues very long.

If you're a guy like me, whose primary talent is hitting singles, you must find other ways to help the club. You have to steal bases. You have to score runs. And you'd better be a good defensive player.

When I first came up I knew there was a lot I could do, but my game needed work. Now I think I've established myself as a well-rounded player. But I still get by on the little things. There's more to success than smacking 200 hits and winning Gold Gloves.

I'm wondering, "How can I pick up an extra 90 feet? How can I move this runner over?" No one pats me on the back when I hit the cut-off man. No one dangles a three-year contract extension in front of me when I back up a base.

But I guarantee you that doing all these little things will make you a better ballplayer at any level, and might just help you make it to "The Show."

If you look at my track record, well, it seems like each year someone says I can't do something. Boom—I go out and disprove them. Most scouts believed I could swing the bat pretty well, but I would bet my house that nobody thought I'd win five Gold Glove Awards for fielding. No one thought I'd steal 50 bases in a year. And people doubted I would ever drive in more than 70 runs in a year. But I've done all these things!

And it didn't come from sitting around; I had to work at my craft.

When you work at something you're going to see results. But you have to believe in your ability. People can heap accolades on you, but you can't work hard to impress other people—you have to do it for yourself.

There will always be little things you can do that other people aren't aware of. You have to make the team aware of those things—it's your responsibility.

Terry Kennedy, our starting catcher in San Diego for many years, would never stand at the plate to field a throw coming into home—he didn't want to risk a collision. He'd run up in front of the plate, catch the ball, and then try to dive back to apply the tag. He just gave it up. He'd often short-hop the ball and throw to second instead of catching the lead runner at the plate.

Benito Santiago will not settle for the easy way out. He'll trick the runner into thinking there's a clear path to home plate. Without warning, Benito will close off the plate by sliding his foot back into position—sort of setting a screen—at the last minute.

Benito helps make my job easier; he puts himself at risk to field my throw and record the key out. Again, it's the little things that win ballgames.

Backing up the bases is a pet peeve of mine. Many guys won't go that extra mile to back up a base.

When I came up as a left fielder, a guy hit a shot down the right field line in one of my first spring training games. The ball went into the corner. The throw from the right fielder sailed over the third baseman's head—and there I was to back up the play.

That play caught Dick Williams's (my manager at the time) attention. I was just a young guy trying to make an impression. And I saved us a run by being at the right place at the right time. A left fielder has to back up the play at third on a ball hit down the right field line—it's part of the job.

Williams brought up the play in practice the next day. He said, "Everybody has to work on cut-offs and relays except for Tony Gwynn; he ran all the way from the outfield to back up at third base. That's the first time I've seen that in five years."

He kept me out of that drill. And I think my attention to detail is what really impressed him about me. Being in the right place at the right time, hitting the cut-off man, picking up the quirks of a pitcher's delivery, rounding the bases correctly, not trying to do too much as a hitter—the little things.

All I ask is that you try to understand the basic principles I'm teaching. As you get older, the concepts and techniques will become increasingly clear to you.

That's my goal in writing this book: I want to make people aware of the proper way to do things. Once you gain experience and move up the ladder, you'll see all these techniques and principles in action. You won't understand everything right off the bat. It's going to take time for you to apply it to your personal style of play.

Ten years from now there will be a new generation of major leaguers. Many of these guys will arrive on the scene as complete players, capable of performing the fundamentals and basic techniques correctly. All they'll have to do is incorporate the little things—the nuances of the game—into their repertoire.

I know that sooner or later one of my students is going to make it to the big leagues. You'll tell everyone that, "Yeah, I'm just putting what I learned from Tony Gwynn into action at the major league level." Now that will be a great feeling!

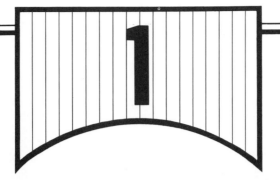

SELECTING THE RIGHT BAT

THE length and the weight of the bat are so important. Let's face it, the size of your bat is going to determine what type of swing you have. If it is too big for you, you're not going to have a controlled, fluid swing.

Grab a bat you can handle with confidence. You don't want your bat to drag through the zone; you want to extend the barrel of your bat out over the plate so you can do some damage.

I believe in using a light bat, what I call my "peashooter." It gives me a sense of control when I step to the plate: I know I can get the bat on the ball and make solid contact.

I discovered the light bat when I was playing at San Diego State University. Before going to college I used any bat that was available—I wasn't too picky.

I hit .301 my sophomore year at State—not bad, but nothing special. I just kind of shook it off as being rusty because I skipped playing baseball during my freshman year.

Coming back the next season, I immediately got thrown into the batting cage to work on my stroke. My old aluminum model from sophomore year (34 inches, 32 ounces) had a big dent in it so I had to find a new bat.

I went into the cupboard at the San Diego State locker room. I was looking around, and found this little 32-inch, 31-ounce bat. I pulled it off the rack and just kind of fiddled with it in my hands and thought, "This bat feels so good; I wonder if I can hit with this thing?"

So I brought it into the batting cage and right away I'm stinging the ball.

A sampling of bat sizes and makes. My Tony Gwynn Louisville Slugger—Model C-263s, 32½ inches long and 31 ounces—is in the middle. Notice how small it is: my "peashooter."

I'm hitting line drives all over the place. From that point on I was so conscious of the length and weight of the bat. Before this I'd never given it much thought. I always believed if a bat felt comfortable in your hands you could go up to the plate and do your job.

The next day we were set to play against UCLA. The game was up in Westwood and Matt Young (now a big league pitcher) was starting. On the ride to Los Angeles all the hitters were talking about how to hit against Young. I mean this guy throws cheese—baseball lingo for a nasty fastball.

I decided to try my peashooter—the 32-inch, 31-ounce bat—in a game for the first time. The results were immediate and amazing. I went 4 for 5 against Young—even though he was throwing cheese and had good control—and hit the ball hard all five times at the plate. Even when I was fooled I could stay back and hit the ball the other way (to left field). I was convinced that I should stick with a shorter bat because I could control it better.

I hit .430 the rest of the season. A lot of people thought I owed this great season to experience—that I had a year of college ball under my belt and was just starting to come around as a hitter. But in my mind, I knew it was the bat. As a matter of fact, I suggested that all my teammates should start using something lighter—I was hitting the ball hard almost every time up at the plate.

I suddenly began to notice the bat size of the other guys on the team. A typical light aluminum model was 34 inches and 29 ounces—that's a big difference between weight and length—while my bat—at 32 inches and 31 ounces—had a much closer ratio of inches to ounces.

The other players were getting whip action with the longer bat, but there wasn't enough weight in it to have a positive impact on their swing. With my 32/31, though, the balls were taking off after they hit the ground; I was getting the action I needed to make consistent contact and put the ball in play.

A lighter bat is better for most hitters, and that's true for both wood and aluminum. Making the adjustment from aluminum to wood is not as difficult as you think; it's simply a matter of getting your hands tough enough to handle the wood.

It takes time. On my very first swing in professional baseball (I was playing for Walla Walla, the Padres Class A af-

filiate in the Northwest League), I hit the ball off the end of the bat, it splintered all over the place, and my hands were on fire. I was begging to have my aluminum bat back.

That fear of the wood didn't last too long, though. I'm a contact hitter, a guy who uses bat control to consistently put the barrel of the bat on the ball. The short, light bat gives me the precise control I need to be successful; whether it's aluminum or wood doesn't make much difference.

It is easier for a contact hitter to go from aluminum to wood than a power guy. Home run hitters are used to getting the barrel of that aluminum bat out in front of the plate, often not smacking the ball squarely, and still hitting it out of the park. With a wood bat you have to be letter-perfect almost every time to drive a ball over the fence.

Stick with aluminum until you have to switch when you make it to the pros. Using the aluminum bat will help you advance to the professional ranks a lot quicker because you can afford to make mistakes and still hit the ball hard. But you have to take a crash course in hitting once you do switch to the wood; you'll really learn a lot about yourself as a hitter—the days of those lucky aluminum bat base hits will be over.

I was scared when I went up to hit for the first time in professional baseball. The Salem Angels had a 6-foot 7-inch pitcher by the name of Buck Long on the mound. He threw 90 mph gas. I remember thinking to myself, "If this guy jams me with an inside pitch, my hands are going to be killing me." When I first got into pro ball I said stupid things like that instead of just concentrating on hitting the ball. But I grew up in a hurry.

When I arrived at Walla Walla the smallest bat they had was 34 inches and 32 ounces—I had to choke up. When you're down in Class A you can't have specialized equipment. The first couple of weeks were tough. I was going through bats pretty quickly. I was getting jammed, not quite extending the barrel enough on the inside pitch to hit the ball to left field.

That first month I was swinging a 34½-inch, 35-ounce bat, choking up on it, just trying to get by. When I brought the problem up to the manager—his name was Bill Brick—it was kind of a shock to him. I said, "Coach Brick, these bats are too big for me; I need something a little bit smaller." And at the time I was hitting about .360.

He told me I had to make the best of it—"You're hitting .360, what else do you want?" I was fortunate that the major league players were on strike that year (1981). So the club shipped me some bats from the Padres, castoffs from the players who'd been traded or released.

In that batch of bats was a box of Mike Ivie 016s. They were too big for me, but the handles were so good that

it was easy to choke up. I used these bats until our club went on the road to Eugene, Oregon.

The Walla Walla Padres had the afternoon off, so Greg Booker, John Kruk and I walked into a sporting goods store in Eugene, casually browsing through the racks of Little League bats on display. And, to my surprise, I found three Mike Ivie 016s, 32 inches and 31 ounces.

I brought my new bats with me to the ballpark the next day and everybody laughed at how tiny they were. But I started using the 32/31s right away, and from that point on I went on a tear. I hit home runs in five straight games, stuff I'd never done before, and that really convinced me that size was important.

With the smaller bat, I could inside-out the ball to left field, handle the inside pitch that used to jam me—even drive the ball over the fence. I hit 12 home runs in a month and a half at Walla Walla; many people thought I'd be the type of hitter who could blast 25 home runs a year. It hasn't turned out that way, of course, but the size of the bat was—and is—very important.

I can talk all day long about what I like, but you're the one who has to try

Using a small bat with balanced weight gives me better control and consistency at the plate.

different things to see what works best for you. Experiment. Vary bat size in baseball practice until you settle on the ideal model. Ask your parents to throw to you while you get the feel of all the distinct styles and sizes.

Go up to the plate with a bat you can handle and control. That's better than using a bigger model, one that allows you to hit the ball well one at bat and poorly the next. The goal is consistency. Whether you're facing a right-hander or a lefthander, attempting to hit a fastball or a curve, you want the same approach—and the same solid swing— every time.

The Tools of the Trade

Select your personal model carefully. I opted for a Louisville Slugger—the first bat company to offer me a contract. I'm loyal to the people who've stuck with me since the beginning.

As soon as I graduated to the majors all the other companies wanted to give me bats. Then when I became successful they really wanted to give me bats. And they wondered why I stuck with Louisville. The answer is loyalty and consistency.

The bats I've used from Worth, Cooper and Adirondack don't feel the same as my Louisville Slugger. Feel is important in the game of baseball. If it doesn't feel right to you, then you're not going to be successful.

I've tried Rawlings and Worth for a game or two. I can be fickle with bats. If my Louisville isn't working for me, and this was especially true early in my career, I'll dabble with an Adirondack. But feel is the key. The Adirondack bats have slick handles, forcing me to apply excessive amounts of pine tar and stickum to improve the grip. Worth bats are always top-heavy.

A Louisville is never top-heavy. Occasionally the handle is too thin or too thick, but the balance is always there. And for a contact hitter like me, balance is the most important quality. Some guys want their bats to be top-heavy; at the point of contact the force is applied in a downward direction on the ball so it will carry farther.

That's not for me. I want balance. Louisville is the one bat with perfect balance from top to bottom. I pull the bat out of the box and I'm sure it's going to be fine.

I've changed models a couple of times during my career. In my first few seasons I went with the K-55, a thick-handled, thick-barrelled bat. But as the 1984 season wore on my bat started dragging, so I switched to a skinnier–handled, big–headed bat to regain bat speed.

For two years I went back and forth: the K-55 during the first half of the season; then the lighter B-267 to increase my bat speed during the dog days of the second half. This plan worked fine until 1986, when I switched to the C-263—Steve Garvey's bat.

I picked up Garvey's bat one day by mistake—thinking it was mine—and it felt good. It was 34/32, an inch and a half longer than my bat, but I liked it.

So I asked Louisville's designers if they could make me a bunch of C-263s.

This became my regular bat from 1986 onward. But in 1988 Louisville discontinued the entire line of C-263s. They said I could have my own model—G-170, the Tony Gwynn special—which was identical to the old C-263.

Well, they sent me these new bats and I stunk for a month and a half. The G-170s were nice looking bats. They felt okay. I just couldn't hit with them. I called the guys at Louisville and asked for a dozen C-263s—32½ inches, 31 ounces.

As soon as the box of C-263s showed up, I hit .360 the rest of the year, and they've been making me C-263s ever since. That's my bat.

Confidence and consistency: that's the payback from selecting the right bat. When you find a bat you trust, one you're really comfortable with, then you won't have to do very much to prepare it for battle.

Rod Carew, a great hitter in the 1960s, 1970s and 1980s with the Minnesota Twins and California Angels, stressed the importance of caring for bats. If you make your living hitting a baseball, sure, you want the best equipment available. But I don't worry about my bats because Louisville has been so consistent. I just apply pine tar and I'm ready to roll.

I use pine tar to enhance my grip. When you get your bat from Louisville, the handle has been sandpapered; this allows you to apply pine tar, stickum or tape. My choice is pine tar with just a touch of rosin on it—that's perfect.

But you have to experiment. Try a few variations to figure out what's best for you.

I'll experiment every now and then. Some of the Louisville bats have too much lacquer—the coat of enamel that makes it shine—so I'll grab a scraper and remove any excess. I might also shave the handles thinner if my hands are sore.

Some guys like to tape their bats and then add the pine tar and rosin. This makes the grip really sticky—you only have to apply the pine tar once or twice during the life of your bat if you use tape.

Grip is the name of the game. You don't want any slippage when you're up there hacking away. Ever see a bat fly out of a hitter's hands? Usually that means the grip wasn't good enough. Other times it's just a guy throwing his bat at the ball in desperation. For me, pine tar, rosin and a pair of batting gloves will ensure a good grip on the bat—and the safety of the fans in the stands.

I didn't start wearing batting gloves until college. I was a dominating hitter in Little League; rarely did I hit the ball on the wrong part of the bat. Since I was making good contact, I never felt the stinging sensation you experience after a bad swing. Yeah, I got blisters with regularity, but once they hardened it was business as usual. Batting gloves didn't seem necessary.

When I arrived at San Diego State, though, batting gloves began to make sense. We were playing Brigham Young University at Provo, Utah, and it was cold. My hands were killing me during batting practice. I did the only smart thing—I borrowed a pair of batting gloves to keep my hands from freezing. I went 4 for 4 despite the cold weather and did some serious rethinking: from that game on I made batting gloves part of my standard equipment.

A dedicated hitter has to hit all the time. When you swing the bat as much as I do it takes longer for the blisters to harden. That's why batting gloves are so important; they'll protect your hands from injury and discomfort. And you get a feeling of confidence when you put your gloves on. You're sure that your hands won't hurt when you swing. What's more, the gloves safeguard your hands as you dive back to first base on a pick-off play or when you slide into the bag.

A batting glove protects your hands from blisters and injury, especially when you are practicing your swing for a long period of time.

All players have their own tastes and preferences in glove design. I prefer gloves that fit snugly; no excess fabric hanging off the end of the fingers for me. And I have small hands, which makes them more vulnerable to abuse.

Franklin gloves are my personal choice; they have curved fingers, forcing the fabric to be perfectly aligned with the natural contours of my hand. Any excess material will allow the gloves to shift as you swing, a great way to raise blisters. You don't want to worry about blisters when you're up at the plate; the idea is to focus on seeing the ball and perfecting your swing.

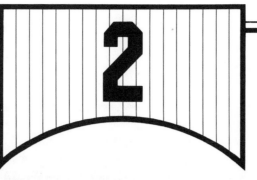

MASTERING RELEASE POINTS

HITTING is an art, one that requires hours of hard work and dedication. Be prepared. Watch that pitcher carefully. The more you know about the guy on the mound, the easier hitting should be.

When a pitcher is warming up in the bullpen, glance down there and study his motion and his delivery. See if he's getting his breaking ball over for strikes. Watch him warm up on the mound before the game and between innings. What's he attempting to do?

As you step into the on-deck circle to take your practice swings, focus your attention on the pitcher. Put your mind in an analytical mode. Consider all the possible things that pitcher will do to mess you up.

But all that analysis ends once you approach the plate. Now it's time to concentrate on the things you know you're capable of achieving.

In the big leagues this whole business is much easier, there's no question about that. You face a pitcher three or four times a year; you study him on videotape. In Little League, high school and college, though, it's hard to recollect what a guy throws. And in many cases you've never even seen him pitch before.

Watching a pitcher go through the lineup should give you an idea of what he might try to do to you. You'll know what his strengths and weaknesses are: is he a cheesemaster or a breaking ball nibbler? If he throws to your

Use your time in the on-deck circle to take practice swings and observe the pitcher.

strengths, take advantage of your opportunity to do some damage; if he pitches to your weaknesses, immediately adjust your approach to combat his strategy.

Name any pitcher in the National League and I can tell you what I'd try to do against him. The book on me hasn't changed that much in the last four or five years. They're going to mix it up, go in and out, change speeds; very rarely will I see a pitch in the same location twice in an at bat.

I would bet you that I know what

their strategy is, but I'm still going to stick with my bread and butter—see the ball and hit it the other way. Unless, of course, the game situation dictates I try something else.

A big league hitter needs to have a game plan. In Little League, though, planning isn't as important. See the ball, take your swing and connect. As you move up the ladder hitting becomes increasingly difficult, because now there's a wrinkle: instead of throwing mostly fastballs, the pitcher is going to toss in a split-finger fastball, curve or changeup. A hitter has to be able to adjust. Again, preparation is

Locate the pitcher's "release point" by focusing on an imaginary box just outside the pitcher's hand. See where I've marked it on Padres' righthander Andy Benes and lefthander Bruce Hurst.

crucial to your success as you advance through the ranks.

Once you've done your homework, it's time for the test to begin. And the actual art of hitting begins with locating the pitcher's release point—an imaginary box somewhere outside of the pitcher's hand. Don't try to follow a pitcher's hand all the way through the windup or you'll get dizzy.

Let's keep it as simple as possible: start by studying the pitcher's face; search for clues to figure out what he might throw. As he's looking in for his signs, you're looking right at his eyes and at the bill of his cap. And then once he begins his wind-up, gradually shift your glance over to his release point, the spot where you think the ball is going to come from.

In 1987 when I hit .370, I was seeing the ball as soon as it left the pitcher's hand. My swing was the same as always. I had the same attitude at the plate. The difference was my ability to pick up the ball right out of the pitcher's hand. With big, slow breaking balls, for instance, I'd stride and just stay there until the pitch got into the zone and then I'd hit it—no problem.

Watch the pitcher to see where he is releasing the ball. His release point will often tip off the pitch. Some guys throw their fastball right over the top and their breaking ball with a three-quarter delivery. That change in delivery might dictate what pitch he's throwing.

Here's what I do: Once it comes out of his hand, I focus in on the ball. I'm not like a lot of hitters who see the ball spin a certain way on a particular pitch.

Fastball grip: across the seams. You'll see white on both sides of the ball.

Curveball grip: fingers placed along the seams, not across them.

I just see the ball. As the pitch is getting close to me, as it comes out of the pitcher's hand and he follows through, I can tell what pitch it is.

Now, I probably couldn't do this during the first week of spring training. Finding release points and identifying pitches demands practice and constant repetition. The more you study a pitcher's release point, the better you're going to be at picking up the ball—what it's doing, where it's going, what the action is, and where it's coming from.

Always watch a pitcher preparing to start his windup. Study him as he assumes his stretch. Check out the grip he places on the ball when he buries it inside his glove.

Most pitchers put the ball into the glove with a fastball grip—you'll see a lot of white on both sides of the ball. One of the easiest pitches to read is a changeup; when a pitcher gets ready to let it go there is very little white showing on the ball.

Many Little Leaguers—and this was true for me as well—get fooled by motion. The pitcher grunts at you like Nolan Ryan, you think it's going to be a fastball, but to your surprise it's a slow changeup. Hang in there. Eventually, you'll learn how to read a pitcher through experience and constant practice.

Even if you're able to read the pitch from glancing at a guy's grip or watching his delivery, you still have to see the ball. I have all kinds of trouble against pitchers who throw with a three-quarter or sidearm delivery. Guys like Dan Quisenberry (a sidearm

Changeup grip: gripped deeper in the hand, so very little white shows when the pitcher is ready to release the ball.

pitcher of the 1970s and 1980s) just wore me out; by the time I picked up the ball it was halfway to home plate. By then it was too late.

During the first half of the 1990 season I couldn't pick up the ball out of the pitcher's hand—I'd say 80 percent of the time I was out on my front foot instead of being balanced and letting the ball come to me. I was repeatedly lunging after the ball instead of staying within myself. This problem all boils down to release points—just see the ball and hit it. Hey, it's hard to believe I hit .309 in 1990 without ever getting into a good groove.

Always remain calm when you're struggling; don't panic and start pressing. Go out and take some extra swings. Watch the pitcher carefully and focus on the little things that signal what he's going to throw. By learning how to locate a release point and focusing on that imaginary box, you'll improve your ability to concentrate at the plate. Once you grasp the concept of the release point, you'll be ready to understand and perfect the mechanics of your swing.

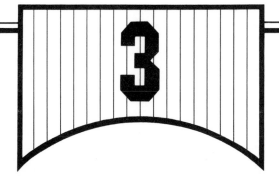

THE MECHANICS OF THE SWING

AN effective swing all begins with confidence. When you're not confident, you start choking your bat and being rigid, almost like a robot. Don't be robotic; when you put your hands on that bat you should be nice and loose.

That's why I move the bat around all over the place; it's what I do to relax. But you'll notice that the moment a pitcher prepares to release the ball, all my movement stops. I assume a position where I'm relaxed and want to attack the ball.

Relaxation is the key to hitting. Your feet and legs must be relaxed; same with the hands and wrists. When you tense up with that lead arm, the swing won't be smooth; it will have a small loop in it. Relaxation brings good things to a hitter.

There are so many little things I do that people wouldn't even notice unless I told them. Like in 1990, for instance, here is what happened: I'd be in my stance. I'd be loose, every part of my body was loose. But as the pitcher released the ball I'd press up with my back leg.

I did that for a month. The hits fell in here and there, but I didn't swing the bat with any consistency. And I think that came from being tense, not having the confidence I needed. I was too concerned with getting my hands through, or trying to pull the ball. When you're nice and relaxed those things don't happen.

The art of hitting begins with a comfortable stance. I like a parallel stance—both of my feet are parallel to each other: I stand in the middle of the box. My front foot is in the front of the plate; my back foot is in the back of the plate. My knees are slightly bent. This is my comfort zone, the one spot I've hit from since my early days of Little League.

I've changed my placement in the batter's box in only one at bat since Little League, just to see what would happen. And what happened promptly brought me back down to earth. I was facing John Franco (then of the Cincinnati Reds) in 1986. I stood in the back of the box and I was so quick on his fastball that I popped it straight up behind the plate—I very rarely foul out to the catcher. That experience taught me to return to my usual spot and stop fooling around.

A comfortable—not viselike—grip is essential to consistent hitting: the middle knuckles of your fingers should be lined up in a row. Some hitters will choke the bat—in which case the middle and lower knuckles are aligned—but it's easier to swing the bat when your middle knuckles are aligned. A

My parallel stance: both feet parallel, in the middle of the batter's box. My front foot is in front of the plate, back foot behind it.

Some players prefer different stances. Here are two examples: standing near the front of the box, and standing near the back. Near the front helps especially when you are bunting for a base hit; near the back gives you a longer look at the pitch.

comfortable grip ensures a smooth swing. Don't squeeze the bat too hard or you'll prevent your muscles from firing properly.

The action of the swing is as follows: I'm in my stance. I'm nice and relaxed. And the first thing I'm looking for is the release point area; then I know to start my movement at the plate.

Movement #1: I'm in my stance. I see the release point and my front foot

A comfortable grip—not too tight—is essential. For proper knuckle alignment, line up the middle knuckles of your fingers on both hands.

A good swing: I'm in my balanced, parallel stance.

Movement #1: I see the pitcher's release point and my front foot lifts up.

When my front foot lands, my hands are back in the hitting position.

goes up. As that front foot goes up, my hands start to go back. And when my front foot lands, my hands are in a hitting position; the rest of my body will stay fixed in its original posture. My stride foot always lands in the same spot every time. And I always land on the ball of my foot—not the heel or flat-footed—every time. The hands/front leg movement is like a trigger: the foot goes up, the hands go back, and when the foot lands I'm in a position to start my swing.

Movement #2: Now the ball is on its way to the plate and I have to determine what pitch I'm going to get and where it's going to be (inside, outside; low or high). The type of pitch and its location will dictate what adjustments I need to make. So when I start to swing, the hips and hands must work together. When I'm in my stance, my weight is balanced; when the hips start to come through the ball, I'm going to shift my weight. As I start my swing, I shift the weight from the back leg to the middle of my body for contact, so my hips and hands come together. I'm

Movement #2: When I start my swing, my hands and hips work together, shifting from the back to the middle to the point of contact.

Movement #3: When I reach the point of contact, my head should be down on the ball; it will look like I'm "watching" it hit the bat.

Movement #4: After contact, I follow through and finish with my hands up high.

shifting my weight from the back to the middle to the point of contact. And I'm swinging down on the ball, as if I was chopping down a tree with an ax.

Movement #3: When I reach the point of contact, my head should be down on the ball. It will appear as if I'm watching the ball hit the bat. Now, I won't actually see the ball hit the bat, but if you take a picture of my swing, it will look like I'm watching the ball make contact with the bat.

Movement #4: After contact and my weight is shifted and my head is down on the ball, then I'm going to follow through and finish with my hands up high.

That's my swing—and I repeat the identical movement every time I come to the plate. I don't care if the pitcher is a righty or a lefty, whether the pitch is a breaking ball or a knuckle-curve. Your swing should be the same every time; it's as simple as that.

One way to ensure consistency is what I call shoulder to shoulder: When you're in your stance your chin is over your front shoulder; after you take a swing, though, it's over the back shoulder.

My swing could work for any hitter. The key is to break each step down into a pattern: the first step is what you do with your front foot and hands—pick up your foot, your hands start to go back and when your front foot lands, your hands should not move any more: they're ready to hit the ball.

As you start your swing, your weight is resting on your back leg; you'll feel the weight shift from back to middle to contact. Your hips head into the ball.

Shoulder to shoulder ensures consistency in your swing.

Your hips and hands are going to come together at the point of contact.

Pivot on the back leg so that the weight can shift from the back to the middle. Your front side should be rigid. And on the follow through, the weight will shift from the middle of your body to the front leg. Just follow through and finish high. When you make contact, your head is down on the ball. When you finish high, your head will pop back up—after you hit the ball, not before! And don't simply swing to the ball—remember to swing through the ball.

Break your swing down and put it back together. That's the way to improve as a hitter. If you watch guys around the National League you can become awfully confused. You see so many styles, players using different techniques. You're going to have to figure out what is best for you. It takes work!

I try to keep it simple. When you add a lot of extras to the mechanics of hitting the whole learning process becomes harder. The easier your swing is to understand, then the better your chances are to make adjustments. It won't be necessary to rework the entire swing if you're slumping—add a little here, take a little away there.

It's like putting the pieces of a puzzle together. Add a piece and take a piece away. You are constantly interchanging the different puzzle pieces, but the basics of the swing will remain the same. I don't care if your stance is open or closed, whether you stand in the front or back of the box, the swing is going to stay the same.

Now it's time to examine the various stances. My stance, as you already know, is a parallel stance, about as simple as it gets. The other two basic stances are somewhat more intricate:

The Open Stance: Your back foot is closer to the plate than your front foot. A lot of hitters will favor an open stance if they're having trouble hitting the inside pitch—they feel the open stance provides them with a better look at the ball on the inside part of the plate.

Open stances are rare in the National League. Jose Oquendo of the St. Louis Cardinals has an open stance: His back foot is on top of the plate; his front foot is wide open; and he stands in back of the box to take a longer look at the pitch. Brian Downing and Junior Felix in the American League are two other

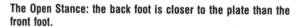

The Open Stance: the back foot is closer to the plate than the front foot.

hitters who use an open stance to get a better hack at the inside pitch.

The Closed Stance: Your front foot is closer to the plate than your back foot. This stance is just the opposite of the open stance—it makes it easier to hit the outside pitch but harder to hit the inside pitch. Rick Dempsey has a closed stance, as does Will Clark of the San Francisco Giants.

Every time we play the San Francisco Giants I stand out in right field and watch Will in that closed stance of his. I always think, "Bust him inside; he can't turn on an inside pitch!" He proves me wrong, though, by smacking that inside pitch with consistency and power.

During the 1989 season, Will didn't struggle with any pitch—he could hit

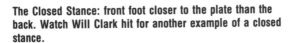

The Closed Stance: front foot closer to the plate than the back. Watch Will Clark hit for another example of a closed stance.

everything. He'd drive the outside pitch to left-center, pure and easy. Before 1989 he could handle the inside pitch but had trouble with the pitch away because he would attempt to pull the ball. Then, in 1990, he reverted to the old Will Clark, always trying to pull—not drive—the outside pitch.

With my parallel stance, I feel it's tougher to hit an inside pitch. But, hey, that's how it works for Tony Gwynn. There could be other hitters with a parallel stance who struggle with the outside pitch.

The point is that no one can tell you what stance to use. I don't force my students to go with a parallel stance, though it's been very successful for me. Keep trying different stances until you find one you're comfortable with.

Practice the mechanics of the swing until it's automatic, almost a reflex reaction. I don't care if your stance is open, closed or parallel. The basics of the swing—stride, push your hands back, hips and hands to the ball and follow through—always remain the same.

KNOW YOURSELF AS A HITTER

O NCE the mechanics of the swing are in place, it's time to figure out whether you're a power or a contact hitter. When a power hitter takes his swing, the path of the bat travels over one-half to two-thirds of the plate. A contact hitter, though, covers the entire plate through the path of his swing.

If you are consistently hitting the pitch out in front, then consider yourself a power hitter. I don't care how big or tall you are; hit the ball out in front of the plate and you'll drive the ball farther than guys who connect at the back of the plate. Even a smaller player like Brett Butler can drive the ball over the fence; he's making contact out in front!

I'm a contact hitter. I hit the ball at the back end of the plate. I spray the ball all over the field. I'll probably never total 20 home runs in a season.

But a contact hitter is not looking for home runs; he's determined to make solid contact, to hit the ball hard somewhere. And sure, when you're growing up and playing Little League, you can connect at the back end of the plate and—thanks to an aluminum bat—still hit home runs.

But as you move up the ladder the issue of power versus contact will form a clear-cut pattern: players who consistently hit home runs are striking the ball in front of the plate; players who hit for a high average make contact closer to the plate. There's nothing wrong with either style. All I ask is that you find a style you like and stick with it.

A power hitter with a .220 average can still be successful if he smashes 35 home runs and drives in 100 runs. Joe Carter of the Toronto Blue Jays is constantly connecting in front of the plate and driving the ball. But when I consistently hit the ball out in front I'm no longer a .220 hitter. The closer I work the pitch to the back of the plate, the better a hitter I'm going to be.

It's just a matter of knowing yourself as a hitter. When you understand what you can do, come to grips with your strengths and weaknesses, you'll go with what works on a consistent basis. My weakness is hitting the ball out in front; that's not something I'm going to emphasize. If a ball is down and in on me, I'll hang back and drive the pitch to left field. It's my way of being consistent.

Consistency is the hardest part of hitting. One year you might handle a certain pitch; the next year you might struggle against the same pitch. But a hitter will have a strength—his forte—and that won't change.

Wade Boggs went from 8 home runs to 24 home runs in one year. But his strength—hitting the ball to left field—didn't change. He made an adjustment to hit for more power—a skill he wasn't as strong in—and he flourished.

Wade is the one hitter in baseball who can do whatever he wants. He can hit home runs and continue to keep his average in the .350 range. There's prob-

Power hitter vs. contact hitter: the bat path of a power hitter covers ½ to ⅔ of the plate, while a contact hitter's bat path covers the entire plate.

ably some determining factor behind his sudden power surge (he went back to being a singles hitter again the following year). The bottom line, though, is that Wade is one of a kind. It is rare when a guy can plan to hit .320 with 20 home runs and 80 ribbies and actually pull it off.

The ability to hit the long ball has its mystique, no doubt about it. Pitchers fear a power hitter more because they know one bad pitch could cost them the game. But you can make your living being a contact hitter. You don't receive the notoriety of an awesome power hitter, but it's a job too. There's an art to contact hitting, and I take a lot of pride in refining that art.

But I understand where a power hitter comes into play in baseball strategy—the slugger is a guy who can turn the game around with one swing of the bat. I've seen that in action the past several years with Joe Carter and Fred McGriff. As they step to the plate, the pitcher bears down more than he would against me—unless I'm hitting with two outs and a runner in scoring position. Then all of a sudden I assume that same aura of fear.

I only fanned 23 times in 1990. The pitcher knows I'm going to get my bat on the ball. He's just hoping the ball will be hit right at someone. So with two outs and a runner in scoring position I play a little mental game: I make believe there's no one on base. That takes some of the pressure off.

A pitcher will respect and fear me with two outs. Of course the fans don't get as worked up as they would with a power hitter. But when a slugger comes up with runners in scoring position and two outs, then I honestly believe that many pitchers—the ones who have confidence in their stuff—would rather face the power guy than the contact guy. The pitcher feels like there are more holes to take advantage of.

A power hitter, remember, is consistently hitting the ball out in front—an area prone to making mistakes. A breaking ball is moving most dramatically just *before* it reaches the plate—so a power hitter is vulnerable to that pitch, while a contact hitter can read the break and hit the ball late, as it crosses the plate. I've been walked countless times with two outs so the pitcher can face Jack Clark, Fred McGriff, Joe Carter or Benito Santiago. The pitcher is certain I'm going to make solid contact—that's a given—so he'll take his chances with whoever is batting behind me.

Don Zimmer, then manager of the Chicago Cubs, walked me intentionally four or five times in 1990 to pitch to Jack Clark. This is fairly typical. I honestly believe that when the chips are down—the game is tied with a runner on second and two outs—a pitcher would rather face a power guy than a contact guy.

Now, I don't want to knock power hitters. Usually, though, a player who hits 25 to 30 home runs will also strike out 90 to 120 times. With 600 at bats and 120 strikeouts, my guess is that there is a hole in that swing. And that's why a pitcher would rather pitch to a power hitter in a two-out, man-on-second situation.

Let me give you an example: The Padres are playing the Cincinnati Reds at Riverfront Stadium. It's the ninth inning of a tie ballgame. Bip Roberts is on second base, the potential go-ahead run. Rob Dibble is on the mound. It's my turn to hit. Jack Clark is waiting in the on-deck circle. In this case, Lou Pinella (the Reds' manager)would walk me to get to Clark—he has more holes in his swing; there's a better chance that he'll strike out to end the inning. But if the closer is a southpaw like Randy Myers, and it's the same situation, he'll pitch to me—it's a percentage move, a question of strategy.

Strategy plays an important part in the game of baseball. A proven power hitter, an Eric Davis, will assume a contact hitting approach at times if the strategy calls for a single instead of a home run. But once again it all goes back to doing what you do best. If you are confident in your ability to put the bat on the ball and go the other way, then take a shot at it.

Rely on your strengths. A hitter shouldn't depend on his second- or third-best skill. It's akin to a pitcher who doesn't want to get beat with his second- or third-best pitch. He'll win or lose with his best pitch, the one he has the most confidence in.

Again, adapt a style that's right for you and stick to it. Know yourself as a hitter! The sooner you learn all the unique qualities of your game—power versus contact, open versus closed stance, and even your personal strike zone—the quicker you'll move up the ladder.

I have a definite point of view about learning the strike zone. From Little League to the big leagues—perhaps with the exception of guys who are 6'5'' or taller—the strike zone is from just above the shin to letter-high. Pitches in that zone are the ones you can hit hard. Anything above or below that zone will be hard to handle.

I'm different than most hitters: My strike zone extends from just above the shin to the letters, but there are certain pitches below the shin and above the letters I can handle.

The quicker you learn your own strike zone—the balls you can handle well—the better off you'll be. And the strike zone does vary from hitter to hitter. It takes constant practice—using the batting tee, taking batting practice, swinging the bat at countless pitches in games—to learn your personal "zone."

You often hear the expression, "getting the ball in your zone." It's really quite simple—wait for a pitch you can hit, and usually that will be a ball in the strike zone.

Work on learning the strike zone! Swinging at the right pitch will become second nature, an automatic reflex. When I go up to the plate I don't worry about the zone. My objective is to hit a pitch I can handle, and there are lots of pitches—in and out of the zone—that appeal to me.

I'm not the best person to talk to about being selective and drawing walks. I like to hack. I like to get my swings in during an at bat. But I'm working out more walks than I used to—I'm somewhat more selective—because I have a better understanding of my strike zone.

A pitch down below my shins? I'll hit that to left field. And I turn on some inside pitches and hit them down the right field line. Again, my strike zone is wider than that of most hitters.

If you glance at Ted Williams's book, *The Science of Hitting*, there is a diagram of the strike zone—it's 7 balls across and 11 balls high. My strike zone, though, is 10 balls across.

If I'm confident I can put my bat on the ball, then I'll swing at the pitch; no doubt about it. I can handle a few more balls than the average hitter, but that's just the way I am. It's an individual thing.

You don't always want to be too aggressive. Avoid swinging at a bad pitch when a guy is struggling with his control. If a pitcher can't find the plate I'm not going to help him out. I'll take a pitch, regardless of the situation. With runners on second and third with no outs—say he walked a batter and then wild pitched him to second or third—I'll take a strike on the first pitch, even if it's a fastball right down the middle.

I'm an aggressive hitter but I often like to give up a strike. In 1984, with Alan Wiggins batting ahead of me, he'd get on and I'd take a few pitches to allow him to steal. I'll spit on the first fastball I see—it doesn't faze me.

Knowing the strike zone is very important. I can't emphasize this enough. Use a tee; hit off a machine that has actual arm action—like the Iron Mike; take BP; face live pitching; do what's necessary for you to understand and perfect your unique qualities as a hitter.

HITTING DRILLS FOR SUCCESS

THE batting tee is the best learning tool; it will teach you what pitches you can handle and what pitches you need to work on. And it will also help to refine your swing.

But contrary to popular opinion, the tee is not home plate; it's simply the hitting area. Kids get in close to the tee as if they were standing at home plate. That's the wrong approach. I'll teach you how to use the tee properly.

Begin with your stance: stand closer to the tee if you want to hit the ball the other way. You'll be at or behind the plate when you make contact. But don't stand right on top of the tee to pull the ball. Move the tee so that when you swing, you'll be able to get the barrel head of your bat out to where the ball is resting.

Once you understand that it's okay to move the tee—it's the hitter who doesn't move—you'll learn more about your strengths and weaknesses. The tee indicates what you do with certain pitches in a particular area. If you stick the tee way out in front and try to hit the ball to left, for instance, you'll have to lunge to make contact. That's exactly what would happen in a game.

Move the tee around to different positions to approximate the different pitch locations. The angle of the bat will determine where you hit the ball.

Begin with your stance; say for the sake of argument it's a parallel stance like mine.

Three things should happen in a typical tee drill: make contact with the ball as you face the tee to hit to left field; make contact with the tee moved slightly forward to hit to center field; and make contact with the tee moved considerably forward to hit to right field. Position the barrel of your bat so that you can accomplish all three goals.

Every swing of the bat follows a distinct arc; my arc is from the outside corner across to the inside corner. Same thing for a righthanded hitter, as

long as he's a contact guy who covers the entire plate through the path of his swing. The tee is on a movable arc that corresponds to the arc of the swing. That's why it is such an effective instructional tool.

Until you show this to kids, though, they don't understand; they just see the tee and think they're supposed to hit the ball. T-ball drives me crazy. You watch these little kids stand right up on the tee, with the coach screaming, "Keep your head down, stand on top of it and try to hit the ball." That advice is not going to help a kid at all.

Education and the basics. Under this

The batting tee is the best way I know to perfect your swing. Use it to develop consistent form and to learn to hit to all fields.

Move the tee to practice hitting pitches in different locations. Here I've moved it forward and slightly outside, to work on hitting to left and center fields.

heading I always include the tee. Strive for correct form. Always try to make contact with the top half of the ball. Polish your swing to hit hard grounders and line drives. Smack the bottom half of the ball, though, and you'll hit it up in the air.

Power hitters are known for hitting those high fly balls. Many true sluggers would rather hit a line drive home run. If the ball doesn't carry far enough, they'll still get a double or triple. Hit

the bottom half of the ball, sending it up on a fly, and eight guys will have a shot at making the out. Line drives are tougher to defend against.

The tee is one of my favorite devices. I've relied on it since playing college ball. And, yeah, I know a standard rubber tee is nothing more than a plate with a pole on it. It's nothing special to look at. Many kids won't stay with it. They'll give it up in a hurry because it's not fun.

But I put a Walkman in my back pocket, slip on my headphones and concentrate on hitting the ball—always making sure my mechanics are correct. I use the music as motivation; listen to Grover Washington Jr. and just focus on getting the job done.

In this day of elaborate gadgets and gimmicks, there's no better buy than a $10 or $15 tee. Grab a whiffle ball, or roll up a pair of old socks, and you're set.

The other drill I recommend to aspiring hitters—one that's a favorite among guys on the San Diego Padres—is soft toss. One player sits with a bucket of balls. He tosses each ball underhanded to a hitter; a net is set up to collect the balls. The tosses cover all parts of the hitting area, forcing the batter to adjust to a variety of pitch locations.

Hitting against soft toss is based on the same idea as hitting off the tee: you

Try to make contact with the *top half* of the ball, to hit hard grounders and line drives.

want to work on smacking the top half of the ball and stroking line drives. Whether you're hitting to left field, right or center, the ball should still end up in the net. Missing the net indicates there's a problem with your mechanics: you're either hitting the bottom half of the ball or not keeping your head down.

The soft-toss drill and the tee are the

best ways to improve your hitting; they're what I believe in. There are other drills I don't care for—one-knee drills, for instance, where the hitter drops down on one knee and just works his top hand. It accomplishes the same thing, basically forcing you to hit the top half of the ball, but it only works the upper half of your body.

As far as special equipment that's designed to assist you with your batting stroke, I recommend the Solo Hitter—a stationary object that compels you to move your feet to adjust to the pitch, depending on whether the ball is inside or outside. You can move the ball up and down, or to the inside or outside corner of the strike zone. The Solo Hitter will teach you what you're likely to do with each pitch in a certain area.

Here is the ideal hitting instructional program for a young player: 100 swings a day, either with soft toss or the batting tee. Take about 20 swings and then move the tee to another area. In the case of soft toss, ask your teammates to throw the ball to a different part of the strike zone after 20 tosses. The ball should consistently end up in the net. Every hit should be a sharp line drive. Always concentrate on hitting the top half of the ball.

Correct form is equally important when using a tee. Correct form means a line drive; bad form means you'll hit the top of the garage or miss the ball completely—or even smash the tee. If

Another hitting tool, Solo Hitter, helps you learn to move your feet to adjust to the location of the pitch.

you hit the tee you're just swinging wildly.

Here are a few common mistakes on the tee: Are you consistently poking the ball onto the roof of your garage? That means you're not hitting the top half of the ball. Taking a cut, only to discover that the ball is spinning off to left field? Yeah, you're probably pulling off the ball. Hooking the ball? The problem is basic—you're getting your top hand over and beating the ball into the ground; the swing is not on a level plane. These are just a few things you can learn from the hitting tee.

Many young hitters think that batting practice and pitching machines are crucial to learning how to hit. Just understanding the basic fundamentals of hitting is more important. A regular $10 tee and three or four whiffle balls will do more for you than all the batting practice in the world could ever do.

Pitching machines can actually do more harm than good. A lot of Little League instructors in San Diego are bragging because they have pitching machines. I always remind young players that a pitching machine has no release point; you don't see the ball until it's already on its way. What sense does it make to get out in front and pull the ball? You'll have to cheat by starting the swing too early.

In this situation I want you to hit the ball the other way. Don't even mess around with pulling the ball. Get comfortable in your stance; see the ball; and

hit it the other way. You have more time to hit to the opposite field. But the kids I talk to don't buy that. They want to believe that it's fine to hit at 70–80 mph off a machine. With the lack of arm action it's like hitting a 100-mph fastball!

Don't try to put yourself in a big leaguer's shoes until you've mastered the fundamentals. Batting practice is a good example. If kids come out to major league games and watch BP they won't learn a whole lot.

Most hitters in BP are trying to smash the ball over the fence. The tendency is to pull the ball right away. In a game situation, though, you'll jam yourself if you pull the ball immediately. Be realistic—in BP the best fastball might "whiz" by at 65 or 70 mph; no problem. But in the game the pitcher is throwing 90-mph cheese— that's a big adjustment the first time you attempt to pull the ball.

My goal in BP is to work with my bread and butter, which is hitting to the opposite field. I start out by trying to hit the left field line as many times as possible. After smoking eight or nine balls to left, I'll start to work my way around the diamond: Hit the pitching screen up the middle; pull the ball into the hole; hit the ball down the right field line.

My personal objective is 200 to 300 swings per day, including batting practice, game swings, cuts in the on-deck circle, soft toss, batting tee drills and hitting in the cage. If I can squeeze in my 200–300 swings, then I'm comfortable, more than ready to do some damage.

Preparation is crucial to success. Take those 100 swings with either the tee or the soft-toss drill. Stay hungry. Be dedicated. Believe in yourself. Think I won four batting titles on sheer ability? Think again.

THE ART OF BUNTING

K NOWING how to bunt has its advantages. Take a look at Brett Butler of the Los Angeles Dodgers. Everybody knows that he's going to lay down his share of bunts. He's going to beat out 20 to 30 bunt hits a year. The third baseman has no choice but to give himself up, play shallow to take the bunt away from Butler. But that won't stop him; he'll bunt anyway.

Bunting adds a different perspective to your game. It gives the other team one more thing to worry about. They have to respect your ability to bunt, so the infielders will move in or over a step in anticipation—that infield shift could open a hole for a base hit.

The Five Most Common Bunts:

Bunt #1—The Sacrifice:

You get the sign from the coach; you know you're giving yourself up to move the runner over. No deception. The pitcher comes to his stretch, you square away to bunt, he starts his delivery to the plate, and you pivot on your back foot. If you're a lefty, your left hand is just below the trademark and your right hand is on the handle. It's the opposite if you're a righty. You want to move the top hand up the trademark. The top hand functions as

The Sacrifice Bunt: pivot on your back foot to face the pitcher, use your top hand to control the bat, and your bottom hand to dictate the direction of the bunt. Here I'm bunting to my right, toward first base.

a fulcrum; the bottom hand dictates the direction of the bunt. And you're just sacrificing, giving yourself up to move a runner over.

Bunts #2 & #3—The Drag Bunt and the Push Bunt:

Both bunts are designed for beating out a base hit. Begin by looking around to see where the first baseman and the third baseman are playing. Dragging a bunt (for lefthanders) means you're going to take the ball with you as you run down the first base line. A right-hander can either bunt the ball down the third base line or push a bunt to-wards first base—you're trying to place the ball between the mound and first base.

That's essentially the same goal of the drag bunt for a lefty—everybody thinks you're supposed to drag it right down the line; in actuality, you want to drag the ball between the pitcher and first baseman. Those guys have to get it together quickly to decide who is going to cover the bag. If there's a split-second of indecision, then you'll beat the throw.

It's the same technique from a right-hander's perspective—when you push the ball between the pitcher and first baseman, you want to capitalize on that moment of confusion.

On the drag bunt for lefties, instead of just pivoting and giving yourself up, you cross over with your back foot. Your left hand is held firmly on the trademark; your right hand is on the handle; and the objective is to place the ball between the pitcher and first baseman.

When a righthander pushes the bunt toward first, the approach is identical—the top (right) hand is held firmly on the trademark, the bottom hand is on the handle—as the goal is to sharply push the bunt to a specific location.

Placement is so important. Lefties can bunt down the third base line, but only if they're adept enough to drop the ball into a little square—sort of a no man's land—between the catcher and third baseman. Brett Butler is the best I've ever seen at doing this consistently. Righties can also drag the ball

The Drag Bunt *(right)*: to drag a bunt, meet the ball out in front of the plate and angle the bat toward third base if you hit righthanded, or first base if you hit lefthanded.

down the third base line—they just push the trademark out there and try to beat the throw.

Bunt #4—The Slug Bunt:

This is a favorite among pitchers. You pretend to be sacrificing. You'll square away to bunt with your hands below the trademark. And all of a sudden you pull the bat back or bring your bottom hand up and literally chop the ball down on the ground.

With a pitcher up, usually the infielders are on the move—the third baseman is breaking in towards home plate, the shortstop is on his way to cover second or third, and the second baseman is going to first or second—

so the hitter pulls the bat back and just tries to chop the ball on the ground because there are holes everywhere. Hit the right hole and this is going to work.

Bunt #5—The Swinging Bunt:

Bip Roberts will do this a lot. Matty Alou made it famous in the 1960s. You offer to bunt, then pull the bat back and take a full swing. You decoy the third baseman into charging towards home plate. The infielders are on the move. And you just put the ball in play. It's a tough bunt to perfect, but very effective if you know what you're doing.

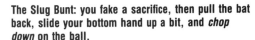

The Slug Bunt: you fake a sacrifice, then pull the bat back, slide your bottom hand up a bit, and *chop down* on the ball.

Learning how to bunt is a big step in the direction of becoming an unselfish player, the type of guy who will give himself up to help his team win. Hitting the ball to the right side of the infield is another unselfish hitting technique.

Some coaches may not agree with me, but I don't think this skill is all that important when you're young. I'm a believer in having fun and mastering the fundamentals before worrying about specialties.

Moving a runner over is a skill that has to be worked on; you can't just go out and do it immediately. Most kids won't feel comfortable with this at first. A righthanded hitter who tries to hit the ball the other way against a righthanded pitcher is going to struggle.

Work on your bunting before you get caught up in the nuances of hitting a grounder to the right side of the infield. A talented bunter puts fear in the other team. Strive for versatility. Prove that you've worked hard to learn the fundamentals. Complete players are rare. Be one of the few guys on your team who can bunt and it will make a difference!

7

HITTING STRATEGIES AND TACTICS

TAKING an awesome fastball and smashing it for a base hit, or even a home run—I know that's something every hitter wants to do. The best advice I can give you is not to change your style of hitting to suit the circumstances. The tendency is to swing harder if a guy is throwing cheese. That's a mistake. The better the mechanics of your swing, the better your chances of hitting the ball.

When I'm facing Rob Dibble or Nolan Ryan, I know they have a great fastball and a great breaking ball. But when they throw the fastball I have to focus on my mechanics, make sure my swing is sound. Rushing the swing is not going to help at all.

It's easier for me to hit against a pitcher who throws 96, 97 mph than a guy who throws 85 mph. The fastball is more of a timing thing—he lets it go, you see the ball, you react. If you're talking about any other pitch—the slider, changeup, forkball, split-finger or curveball—you have to wait.

Adjusting to hitting a breaking ball is not as tough as you think. When I saw a curveball for the first time (this was back in high school), I remembered something Willie Davis—my favorite baseball player—said: "You have more time to hit a curveball than a fastball." When Willie made that statement, suddenly it dawned on me, "Okay, I just have to wait."

Whenever you prepare to swing the bat, in your mind you think it's a fastball. Once you see it's not a fastball you have to wait. A pitcher lets go of the fastball and—snap—it's right on top of you. He lets go of the breaking ball and—snap, snap—it takes a little longer to get to you. It's one extra snap that you need to hesitate before hitting the ball.

With the fastball, it's bring the bat back and swing. When you see anything else, though, it's bring the bat back and wait. Wait for the breaking ball; the same goes for the slider. If a pitcher throws me a slider on the outside part of the plate, for instance, I'm going to get ready, then hit it.

Now the forkball and the split-finger are the toughest pitches to handle. The split-finger starts out with the action of a fastball and suddenly begins to drop—the bottom falls out. But the approach to hitting it is the same: You see it, you wait, and then you swing.

A typical split-finger pitch is down in the strike zone. I often see the split-finger at the bottom of my personal strike zone—down at the shins—and it's hard to handle. The best advice I can give on a pitch down in the strike zone is to hit it the other way—don't try to pull the ball or you'll beat it into the ground.

Sliders pose similar problems. Most pitchers—especially righthanders—won't throw me a slider for a strike.

They'll bury the pitch on the inside part of the plate. And once again, if you're going to pull that pitch—hit it squarely—your timing has to be perfect. A good down-and-in slider is a ball I often foul off my front foot. I'm a little too late with my swing. So I just try to put the bat on the ball and make good contact.

Down and in is my weak zone. This is particularly true of hitting against a righthanded pitcher. When a lefthander throws a slider, though, he's working right to my bread and butter, which is down and away. I can wait on a down-and-away slider and drive it into left field.

The only problem is recognizing whether it's a slider or a breaking ball. From a lefthander there's that fear factor when he snaps a breaking ball in on you—if you flinch on it you're history. If you consistently wait that split second on breaking balls—it doesn't matter which side a pitcher throws from—you'll pick up the break and make the necessary adjustments.

But if you step up to the plate and you're thinking about getting hit by a pitch, then you can't make that judgment quickly enough. When I go up there I'm thinking about distinguishing between the slider and the breaking ball. If I figure out which one it is and wait that split second—boom, that pitch is going to be smoked into the gap.

Most young hitters have problems with pitchers who throw from the same side. This is especially true of lefties like me. Righthanded hitters see so many righthanded pitchers in Little League that they stop worrying about it after a while. But lefty-lefty is different—that fear factor is always an issue.

During the 1990 season there were so many lefthanders with good breaking balls that I found myself flinching a lot. Patience is the solution. Don't flinch. Wait back on the ball and just hit it. It's easier than you think.

I call it not giving in. He might start that breaking ball right at me, but if I don't give in, then it's easier to hit. That's why recognizing the pitch is so important. Pick up the pitch right out of his hand, see what it is and then you'll know whether to wait or go and get it.

Consistency is the secret to success—in baseball or anything you do in life. I always tell hitters to be aggressive, whether the count is 0–2 or 3–0. If the pitcher gets ahead 0–1 it won't change my strategy as a hitter. When I fall behind in the count I'm not going to change.

The goal is to be aggressive, but within reason. If a pitcher throws you a fastball on the outside corner, and you try to be aggressive and pull the ball, you're defeating the purpose. Go with the pitch. Let the ball dictate what you'll do—regardless of the count. Look for a good pitch to hit and attack it.

Don't waste time. A belt-high fastball on the first pitch? That's a ball you want to drive. Try not to waste your opportunities early in the count. You might not see another good pitch to hit in that at bat.

As you advance up the ladder, though, you'll notice a lot of hurlers won't throw you a fastball down the middle on the first pitch. In college you see a lot of garbage early in the count. Then they have to come in with a strike and you can capitalize on that.

I didn't notice any of this until my final year of college ball. I never really paid attention to what a pitcher would do when ahead or behind in the count; it didn't matter because I was always the same type of hitter. But you start picking up these little things and they make you a better player.

Orel Hershiser will not give in. He'll force you to hit his pitch whether he's ahead or behind in the count. Just because it's 2–0 doesn't dictate he's going to throw you a fastball right down the middle. He might, but I wouldn't count on it. It doesn't pay to be aggressive against a pitcher like Hershiser; he'll throw you a dead fish on 2–0 and you ground out to second to end the inning. He kills me.

Don't worry too much about working the count—unless the situation dictates otherwise. If you're behind in the game and it's the last inning, then try to work the count; make him pitch to you. But if it's the third inning of a scoreless game, then see the ball, get a good pitch to hit and go for it.

Much has been said about my use of videotape, how I view tapes before each game to scout pitchers and make adjustments. It's true. I'm a believer in the importance of analysis. I want to know what a pitcher will do to get me out.

Now I understand you're probably not in a position to tape your games. But it's your responsibility to keep track of the pitcher's strategy: Is he throwing the ball in on your fists or trying to paint the outside corner? Is he changing speeds more than he used to? What pitches are working against you? What are his weaknesses? That's the type of information that can help you as a hitter.

Pitchers are like hitters; they try to make adjustments. Take Pascual Perez, for instance. I used to tear him up. He'd throw me fastballs and sliders and I hit the ball really well. Then all of a sudden I went through a stretch where I couldn't buy a hit against him for 12 or 13 at bats. He made an adjustment; he stopped relying on the fastball/slider combination.

So I checked the video to see what he was throwing and discovered a whole assortment of strange pitches—slow curves, lollipop changeups; you name it, he threw it. By looking at the tape I was able to adjust to his pitch selection and location.

Analyzing the tapes also helped me out against John Smoltz of the Atlanta Braves. Smoltz can be pretty nasty. He has a good curveball, a good slider and is working on a changeup. I've been successful against him, though, because I head to the plate with a plan. If he pitches me away I'll hit the ball to left; if he busts me inside I'll turn on it; and if I can't turn on it I'll stick to my bread and butter and inside–out the ball to left field.

I'm pretty perceptive. I don't miss that much, especially when a guy is on the hill. And the quality I always search for is composure. When a guy makes a great pitch and you foul it off, what does he do? Does he freak out on the mound? A lot of pitchers are solid. They don't display much emotion. They stay within themselves.

I'm the same way. I try not to display any emotion, or reveal what I'm thinking. But I'm not beyond showing frustration. When I get a good ball to hit and I don't make contact, I'll look up into the crowd and think, ''God, how did I miss that pitch?''

In the last game before I hurt my finger in 1990, I came up with runners on first and second and two out. Smoltz was throwing me everything in the book—change ups, curves and nasty sliders. I'm beating them in the dirt, fouling them off my foot. But I'm hanging in there. I'm battling tough. He's wondering what he has to do to get me out.

He throws me a change up and I just wave at it. Then I see a breaking ball and I'm out in front, guessing fastball, but I keep my hands back and just flick the ball into right-center. Ron Gant dives, barely missing the catch. The ball finds the gap and rolls all the way to the wall. I knock in two runs with a stand-up triple.

As I get to third base Smoltz has the ball and he's circling the mound, disgusted with himself. I see that and don't react. But I file it away in my notebook and maybe next year it will come into play again.

The little things make a difference.

It gives you confidence to know you've unnerved the pitcher. Messed with his mind. He's more prone to make a mistake when he's not focused on his job.

This is very true of Little League and high school baseball. You see guys—both pitchers and hitters—losing their composure. A tough call or a bad pitch can ruin a pitcher's mental edge. It's up to you to work that to your advantage.

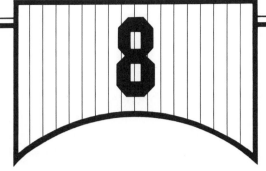

8

TONY GWYNN'S TOP 10

YOU can learn a lot from failure. Why do you struggle against some pitchers? What makes them so tough to hit? I'm always looking at the video, and watching in the game, to pick up the little nuances that will give me an edge.

Here's my list of the 10 toughest pitchers to hit against in the National League. Good pitch selection. The ability to change speeds. The awesome cheese—these guys know how to pitch!

After I analyze each of the top 10 pitchers, I'll explain my strategy in hitting against them. Try to apply my experience to your own unique situation

as a hitter. Remember, no matter how effective a pitcher is, it's still your job to find a flaw, an opening that will enable you to be successful. It's a challenge worth accepting.

1) John Franco (New York Mets): Good sinking fastball. Good change-up—he turns it over. Good breaking ball. While pitching for Cincinnati a few years ago he wasn't afraid to throw any pitch at any time in the count—that's why I struggled against him. He'd fall behind 2–0 and throw a curveball, slider or changeup for a strike. If a guy mixes up his pitches—if he gets ahead on fastballs and suddenly throws four straight breaking

John Franco. *(New York Mets)*

balls—he'll be tough to hit. That's the case with Franco.

2) Orel Hershiser (Los Angeles Dodgers): Another guy who won't give in. He won't say, "Here is a fat pitch; just take your best shot." He won't do that. He'll make you hit his pitch. He has a good sinker. I call it a dead fish. He'll fall behind 2–0, throw a mediocre

fastball with good downward movement, and it's like hitting a rock—it won't go anywhere.

Hershiser is a gamer. With men on base he won't change his approach. No one on base or the bases are loaded, it doesn't matter; he won't change; he's going to pitch his game.

It's extremely difficult to make solid

Orel Hershiser. *(Los Angeles Dodgers)*

contact against him, especially when he's down in the strike zone. When he's down you can just about forget it. You might get lucky and hit a 19-hopper through the infield. But a contact hitter like myself will struggle with a Hershiser—I'm not looking for lift; I'm looking to line the ball somewhere. And against a low-ball pitcher like Orel that is very hard to do.

3) Dwight "Doc" Gooden (New York Mets): Overpowering stuff. Good fastball. Good curveball. Messes around with the changeup. And that pitch is only going to improve as he gains experience.

What I like about Gooden is that with no one on he's fluid and deliberate;

Dwight "Doc" Gooden. *(New York Mets)*

he's not trying to overthrow the ball. He's throwing strikes, putting the pitch where he wants. But when people get on he can turn the intensity up a notch. He rears back and throws you that high-rising fastball whenever he needs a big pitch. With men on base he becomes a lot harder to hit.

I've seen teams in the NL East knock him around. The Padres don't see him as much as the NL East teams so perhaps they know something we don't know. In an average year we'll face Doc two times, perhaps three. We haven't had much success against him, I know that.

4) John Tudor (formerly of the St. Louis Cardinals): He changed speeds

John Tudor. *(St. Louis Cardinals)*

very effectively. I had some success against him, but he was extremely tough. He went in and out, up and down, changed speeds, took a little off the breaking ball, then took a little more off the breaking ball.

You had to wait against him. With most pitchers the difference between the fastball and the breaking ball is one snap of the fingers. But with John it could have been two—or even three—snaps. His fastball topped out at 83 mph, but his change varied: 71 mph on one pitch, 67 on the next and 63 on the one after that. If you geared up for the changeup, he'd slip in that 83 mph fastball and it was right on top of you before you could react.

Sid Fernandez. *(New York Mets)*

It was either feast or famine against Tudor—I had great nights or nothing. Early on, when he first came into the NL with Pittsburgh, I had a couple of good nights against him. But after he went to St. Louis—the season he went 21–8—I could not touch him. He'd run the fastball in on me and break my bat, then he'd throw that slow breaking ball and get me waving at it.

He was extremely frustrating to hit against. You knew he wouldn't pound you with a fastball. But he was so crafty with that breaking ball—so effective with the slow-change—that it would just drive me up a wall.

5) Sid Fernandez (New York Mets): His release point is the problem. He has a good fastball and a good breaking ball, but if he threw from over the top

Tom Glavine. *(Atlanta Braves)*

it would be much easier to see the pitch.

You have to lay off the high cheese when you're facing Sid. Just look for the release point and hope you can see the ball heading down in the zone.

6) Tom Glavine (Atlanta Braves): He has four or five different pitches. Good changeup, but he doesn't throw it enough. I've said that for a couple of

years now. Good curveball. Good slider—he can turn it over and run it in on your hands.

I'm always looking for the hard stuff off of him. The changeup doesn't even cross my mind. But he struck me out a couple of times with that pitch. He has good stuff, sound mechanics and outstanding motion on all of his pitches.

Rob Dibble. *(Cincinnati Reds)*

Glavine is a bulldog. He's a tough son of a gun. He won't give in and will make you hit his pitch.

7, 8 & 9) The Nasty Boys—Rob Dibble, Randy Myers (San Diego Padres) & Norm Charlton (Cincinnati Reds): Dibble and Myers are a couple of gunsmokes. They can bring it up there in a hurry. Dibble is the hardest thrower in the National League, no question about it. He threw harder than anybody I saw last year. He just rears back and lets it go. And he's crazy enough to keep you on your toes—you never know what he might do.

Fortunately, I met him when he first came up to the big leagues. Every time he arrives in San Diego or I go to Cin-

Randy Myers. *(Cincinnati Reds)*

cinnati we talk to each other. He's a good guy. But on the hill he's pretty intimidating. As you step into the box you have to put that intimidation factor aside and think about seeing the ball.

Dibble has a good fastball. Great slider. Better than average sinker that he'll throw three-quarter delivery against righthanders. Just good stuff.

And Myers is the same way. He is not as scary as Dibble, but is still intimidating. Overpowering fastball. Good slider. Good curveball. When you think of Myers and Dibble you focus on the cheese. You don't think about the breaking stuff, but it's there. And they will set up their breaking balls with fastballs and get you out with

Norm Charlton. *(Cincinnati Reds)*

those pitches. The Padres just got Myers in a trade for Bip Roberts; I'll miss Bip, but I'm glad I won't have to face Randy anymore.

Charlton belongs on my Top 10 because he has good stuff. How effective he is, though, depends on whether he's starting or relieving. When Charlton is used as a starter you get three or four chances to adjust. By the third at

bat some of his cheese is gone and he's easier to hit.

I guarantee that I haven't gotten a hit off Charlton in my first two at bats against him. Then in the third and fourth at bats it's a new ballgame. If Charlton stays in the bullpen he'll be nasty; as a starter he definitely loses some of his effectiveness.

10) Dennis Martinez (Montreal

Dennis Martinez. *(Montreal Expos)*

Expos): Martinez is sneaky. He's sneaky because he has at least six pitches and is not afraid to throw inside—he doesn't care who you are. He will bust you off the plate so he can set up what he wants to throw. You could be Mickey Mantle coming out of retirement and he'll still move you off the dish with an inside fastball.

Martinez has a good curveball and fastball. Good screwball, which acts like a tailing fastball—it tails away from a lefthanded hitter with a lot of movement. Good breaking ball.

He throws a variety of pitches for strikes, but the key is that bulldog mentality: he'll do whatever he wants without worrying about who you are. He'll set you up, brush you off the plate and then get you out.

Bobby Bonilla and I were talking with Dennis at the 1990 All-Star Game at Wrigley Field. Bobby was saying, "Man, you ain't afraid of pitching inside." And Dennis said, "No, you can't be." And I said, "Yeah, you've dusted me off a couple of times this year and I know you're not trying to hit me; you're trying to work your game plan." Martinez agreed: "That's right; you can't win in this league unless you pitch inside."

Martinez is the one guy in the National League who is not afraid to pitch inside. Other pitchers who get ahead 0–2 will waste one in the dirt or throw it high. Dennis will come inside and let you know he'll back you off the dish to get you out. I give him a lot of credit.

These 10 pitchers have gotten me out pretty consistently over the years, though I hit close to .300 against Tudor.

I'll only see Franco and Myers—both lefthanders—for one at bat, usually late in the game; ideally with guys in scoring position.

With Franco, I'm just looking for a pitch I can hit the other way. I'm not going to attempt to pull the ball. Same thing with Myers. If it's the last three innings of a tight ballgame, I'm not going to see an inside pitch—inside is the no-no zone for relievers.

I'm thinking: if I can get a pitch up in the strike zone and on the outside part of the plate, hey, that's my bread and butter. I'll hit the ball to left. That's how I've been successful against Myers and Franco—I look for the pitch up and away and drive it to the opposite field. If I get anything inside it will be late in the count, an inside fastball designed to get me out.

Now Charlton is somewhat different. He's not afraid to throw any of his pitches to any location at any point in the count. He's got a forkball that acts like a curveball—first it's up and then it's down. It's a struggle.

But you can't give up on yourself when you're in a bind. Pull up your bootstraps and say, "I know this is going to be difficult, but I'll give it a shot."

Charlton is nasty early in the game. He has movement on his pitches, a lot of action—but as the innings add up he loses some steam on the fastball and the breaking ball doesn't move as much. All of a sudden he's easier to hit. So with Charlton the key is patience.

Don't panic against a guy if you're 0 for 2 and struggling. Don't start worrying about an 0 for 4 washout. It's easier to hit Charlton as the game progresses, and that's true of many starting pitchers—especially the ones who make a living throwing cheese.

Fernandez and Glavine are left-handed starting pitchers. Sid was like Charlton: he'd tire out as the game went along. But during the past few years he's been tough on us all nine innings—he keeps pumping that fastball without letting up.

Again, the key to hitting Sid is finding his release point. Locate his release point consistently and you'll be effective—regardless of which pitch he throws. If he's deceptive enough and can hide the ball he'll get people out.

Glavine is one of those stubborn guys you have to battle. If you go 1 for 4 you've had a big night. He's got good stuff, movement on all his pitches. He doesn't wear out as the game goes along. He'll make you earn whatever you get. Much like Orel, he'll never pump up a fastball and say, "Here it is, try to hit it." He'll change it up to keep you off balance.

My strategy with Sid and Glavine is take them the other way. Charlton is probably the only lefthander in this bunch I'd try to pull because his pitches move in on me. But Charlton is not afraid to bust me inside and run the fastball in on my knuckles. Glavine will run a fastball in on my knuckles and then come back with a slider away, which I try to poke into left field. So with Glavine I have to battle, just take what he gives me and hope I can come away with a decent night.

Tudor is Mr. Changeup. He won't throw a fastball for strikes. He'll show me a fastball inside or up in the strike zone. But he'll try to get me out with the breaking ball and the changeup. I have to be patient, wait for a changeup or breaking ball I can time.

Hershiser, Gooden and Martinez are bulldog types; they'll execute their game plan regardless of circumstances. They'd rather walk you than give you a fat pitch. Doc will occasionally challenge a hitter: He'll say, "Here's my best cheese, let's see what you can do with it." Not many hitters can beat him at this game. I know I can't. I'll take his cheese and try to fight it off to left field.

For Hershiser and Martinez, though, movement is the secret to their success. If they're sharp and have good movement on their pitches, whew, it's difficult to make solid contact against them.

Orel was unhittable in 1988 because of the way his pitches would move. Nothing was straight. The fastball would start in and tail back over the plate or start outside and break back inside. The changeup moved all over the place; the sinker dropped off the table; the breaking ball had that snap. When he's on—and healthy—Orel is as tough as any starter in baseball.

These 10 guys are the best pitchers I've faced in the NL. As tough as they are, I'll stick with my game plan. Stay with your strengths, regardless of who is pitching against you. Believe in your ability to be successful and the hits will come.

THE INNER GAME OF BASEBALL

BASERUNNING is what I call the inner game; it's all psychology—reading the pitcher and maintaining your own aggressive attitude. Be the aggressor. Put the pitcher on the defensive. Distract him from making a good pitch. Always look to take the extra base.

Let's discuss the ideal running form as you round the bases, beginning from the end of your swing at home plate. Say you just hit the ball to the outfield, a tweener into right-center. Here's how you should run down the line: your arms are in an L-shape and in close to the body. The upper half of the body has a good forward lean. Use your arms to pull your body along. Put one foot in front of the other. Run as fluidly as possible.

Take a straight line to first base until you reach about 5 to 10 feet from the bag, then make a small loop, hitting the inside corner of the bag with good body lean. Again, anticipate that the outfielder will bobble the ball, allowing you to continue on to second.

If you're rounding first and you notice an outfielder is moving away from the bag he has to throw to, consider gambling on going to second. For every single you're thinking double. If he misplays the ball or it pops out of his glove, you'll make it to second base—but only if you're running at top speed.

My premise is to always get the extra

Running to first base: arms in close and bent, upper body leaning forward.

Rounding the bag: make a small loop, hit the inside corner of the base, and think about second. Force the outfielder to make you stop.

bag. Be aggressive. If you hit an infield chopper, just run down the line as hard as you can. Same approach with a ball hit to the outfield—there's no guarantee he'll field it cleanly or make an accurate throw.

As you're rounding first base I want you to think about second. You'll know by the time you're two steps around first whether or not you can make it to second safely. If the outfielder handles the ball cleanly, just put on the brakes and head back to first. If he boots it, though, you already have momentum pushing you toward second—you might be able to beat the throw.

You're thinking one bag ahead. If you hit a ball into the gap, for instance, you're thinking three bags. Until the outfielder does something to change your mind, you keep going.

If I hit the ball to the gap in right-center I'm contemplating an inside-the-park home run. I'll be at second by the time they field the ball because the defense is shifted way over to left— that's how they play me. When I hit second base I'm looking at the third base coach and wondering, "Is he going to send me or hold me at third?" Run hard the whole way, whether it's a single, double or triple. If you make sharp cuts around the bags you'll grab that extra base.

Chris Sabo of the Cincinnati Reds is the model baserunner. A routine single and he's thinking two bags. A two-hopper that's hit right at me and he's thinking double; he'll come around the bag hard and if you don't charge the ball he'll take the extra base on you.

It's just a mental thing. You know in your own mind whether or not you can take the extra base. Very rarely have I been thrown out trying to stretch a double into a triple. I tend to make my baserunning mistakes in a steal situation, not on a ball I've hit.

I'll get brain lock in basestealing situations because I think too much. Stealing should be instinctive, not a mental ordeal. Trust your eyes and react. Let your reactions take over. Just from watching carefully I noticed that Jose DeLeon, a pitcher with the St. Louis Cardinals, tips off whether he is throwing to home or first base. He'll come set, nod his head three times and then go to the plate. It's very quick; you have to really pay attention. If he comes set and doesn't do anything, then he's throwing to first.

Now, I preach trust your eyes. But in 1990 I'd be on first, DeLeon would come set and nod his head three times. My eyes were telling me to go but my mind said, "What if? What if he's changed his signal to four nods?" My

Full stride running to second base.

The Basic Lead: find a spot where you are comfortable, but where you can get a good jump toward second without getting picked off base.

eyes were right and my brain was wrong—he still went to the plate.

That's why I say trust your eyes and react. You need to pick up on the little things—the inner game—if you want to steal bases. Trust your eyes and react. If you can do that consistently, then you're going to be a better base-runner, a better fielder, a better thrower and a better hitter.

Being aggressive is the key to so many aspects of this game, especially stealing bases. Lou Brock said a base-stealer has to be fearless; you can't be afraid of getting thrown out. Rickey Henderson, Tim Raines and Vince Coleman have all said the same thing—don't be afraid to fail.

Once you establish an aggressive mental attitude, you can turn your attention to correct technique.

The Basic Lead: Assume a lead that allows you to get a good jump, without putting yourself at risk of being picked off if the pitcher throws to first. I count out 4½ steps off first base. From that position, if the pitcher throws home I can steal second; if the pitcher throws to first I can cross over and dive back into the bag safely. Try it yourself and see how far you can go past the bag without being in that no man's land, the point where you know you're dead meat if he throws over.

As you're leaving the bag there are two things you do not want to do:

never cross over your feet as you come out for your lead. Never walk off the bag with your back to first base. Here's why: If your legs are crossed over each other as the pitcher makes his throw to first, forget it; you'll never get back to the bag ahead of the throw. Same thing with walking off the bag with your back to first; to return to first you have to cross over and you'll be picked off easily.

The One-Way Lead: I use this to study a pitcher's move, test the limits of his concentration. I'll take my safe 4½ step lead. Then I'll add an extra step. That's 5½ steps—a pretty big lead. But I want to see how far I can go before the pitcher will make his move to first. You'd be surprised how many pitchers do not want to throw to first. Remember, they're busy focusing on getting the hitter out. When I get to first a lot of pitchers don't pay attention. They think, "He's not going anywhere." You try to work that being-taken-for-granted stuff to your advantage.

The Pop-up Slide: You need a good feet-first slide to complete your steal. I favor the pop-up, or figure-four, slide. I believe that the quickest way to the bag is the best way to steal. And the pop-up slide is always the quickest way to go.

The One-Way Lead: Add an extra step to challenge the pitcher to throw to first. See how far he'll let you go.

Let's break this whole process down into its simplest form: Take your 4½ step lead. Sprint 10½ steps to second base (you'll be three steps from second) and begin to break down toward the ground—get as low and flat as possible so you'll be sliding—not flying—into the base.

Tuck one leg under and point the other leg straight for the base. Both of your hands are up in the air. (My hand alignment is somewhat unusual; my left hand is up and my right hand is dragged in the dirt—I wear protective straps to prevent my right wrist from getting jammed.) As you reach second, lean forward and use your bent leg to push up. My arms look like I'm grabbing for a pole. Your arms actually help your legs get through the slide—it's the scientific whole-body approach.

The pop-up slide is aptly named— you can pop right up and continue on to the next base in case of a poor throw. I've never been a head-first diver or a hook slider—I believe in a get-to-the-bag-as-quick-as-you-can type of slide.

Pop-up slides are especially useful when you're sliding into home plate. Never slide head-first into home plate! You'll get creamed. Mike Scioscia of the Dodgers is a master of the home plate collision. He takes pride in blocking the

The Pop-up Slide: break down toward the ground and get low and flat.

Tuck one leg under and point the other straight for the base. Hold both hands in the air to avoid jamming them.

As you reach second, lean forward as you slide and use your bent leg to push up. Now you're ready to head for third!

plate. Here's a brief rundown of three head-on encounters I had with Scioscia in the '84, '85 seasons. I was safe all three times, but it was a painful experience.

Collision #1: He dropped the hammer on me and I never got near the bag. I was lucky the ball short-hopped him and I managed to sneak my hand in on the plate.

Collision #2: I tried to go around him and he caught me with his cleat; I tripped over him and sprained my wrist. I was stuck playing with a sprained wrist for a month.

Collision #3: My foot was under him but he dropped the hammer down on my shin. When those shinguards hit your shin—boom, it's a bad feeling.

Believe me, the pop-up is the best slide. You see a Pete Rose, Bip Roberts or Vince Coleman flying in head first and it looks like fun. But it's dangerous. You can get your wrist caught or jam your shoulder.

Stealing Third Base: My initial lead off second is slightly longer than it was off first. The pitcher has a harder throw to pick me off. To complete the play he has to whirl, throw and hit a fielder—either the shortstop or second baseman—on the move. As the pitcher goes to the plate, then, I assume a secondary lead—the position I need to be in to score on a base hit.

You never want the pitcher to know you're going to steal. This is particularly important when stealing third base, because often they're not expecting it. If you give yourself away you'll have the shortstop and third base coach screaming at the pitcher to look at you. It blows the whole deal.

I'm Mr. Aggressive when I get to second base. I take advantage of the element of surprise. And consider that the pitcher is trying to get the hitter out; it's up to you to make the most of your opportunities.

Reading the Pick-Off Move: You need to do your homework if you want to steal bases. If you study a pitcher enough, find out what kind of move he has, you're going to be more successful stealing on him. Even in Little League, believe it or not, there are certain things a pitcher will do when he's going to throw home or throw to first.

Bruce Hurst, a hurler for the Padres, is a good example of how pitchers will telegraph their intentions. Standing out in right field I can tell whether he is going home or to first—when he goes home he has a little leg buckle; when he throws to first he just lifts his leg and throws over to the bag. I don't know if the runner can see that from first base, but I can see it from where I am in right.

So I told him to be consistent—either buckle his leg all the time or keep his leg still all the time. Pitchers are creatures of habit. They do things a certain way. And a lot of times they're not even aware of what they're doing.

As you learn to read the pitcher's pick-off move, you'll learn just how far you can lead and still able to dive back safely. (Here's where a batting glove helps to protect your hands.)

It isn't easy finding the quirks in a pitcher's motion. You just have to keep looking. But it's the little things that help you get to the big leagues—being able to steal at will, for instance. Anything you can do to make yourself a better ballplayer is worth a shot. It's not cheating. It's right there for you to see. It's right there for you to use. And if you can use it to your advantage, why not?

All kinds of information can help you steal a base—the pitcher, the catcher, stealing signs. When we play the San Francisco Giants we've even been able to steal the signs from Roger Craig (the Giants manager). Here's what happened:

First of all, you have to keep in mind that Roger—not the pitcher or the catcher—calls every pitch thrown by every pitcher on the Giants. He flashes the signs in from the dugout to deter-mine the specific pitch, its location, everything. Well, Greg Riddoch (who was a coach at the time) stole their signs.

Riddoch told me that whenever Roger does one thing, the pitcher will throw to first, and when he does something else, the pitcher will throw home. I'd be on first base, look right in at Roger—I didn't even look at the pitcher—and broke for second right after the pitcher lifted his leg.

You're always playing for an edge. I've never been a guy who could steal successfully on 80 percent of my chances. I'm more in the 55–60 percent range. But over the years I've gotten a lot smarter. I have average speed and pretty good quickness—but I need that edge.

Quickness is essential to all players in the stealing game: the runner needs quickness to get a good jump; the

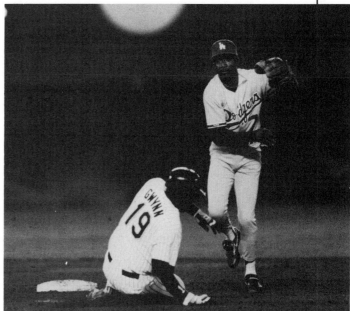

catcher needs a quick release to get the throw down to second; and the pitcher needs a quick pick-off move to first.

The Padre coaches track release time from pitcher to catcher and from catcher to second base—the total time for both throws is usually about 3.5 seconds. If I can go from my lead to second in under 3.5, then I should beat the throw.

Every now and then you'll get a guy like Rick Reuschel (he always pitches from the stretch without a windup), who releases the ball to home plate in 1.4 seconds. That gives the catcher two seconds to throw down to second base—two seconds is a lot of time!

A different kind of slide into second. Here I'm trying to break up a double play by sliding slightly *off* the base, to make the infielder jump to get out of my way, and possibly hurry his throw.

Pitchers with big leg kicks are easy to run on. When they lift that leg you know they're going home. All you have to do is work on getting a good jump.

Pitchers are becoming more deceptive. They've developed the slide-step to get rid of the ball in a hurry. The slide-step: a pitcher comes to the set position; instead of lifting his leg and throwing home, he'll eliminate the leg kick and either deliver the pitch or quickly throw over to first.

A guy like Rick Sutcliffe went from 1.8 seconds (elapsed time from pitcher to catcher) to 1.3 seconds by using a slide-step. Add to 1.3 the two seconds it takes a catcher to get his throw down to second—3.3 in total—and you're going to need a great jump to beat the throw.

That half a second Sutcliffe saves on his release to the plate is crucial. I'm into second easily if he takes his full windup. With the slide-step, I've got one more thing to think about—a good throw is going to nail me.

Catchers are cutting down on their release time too. They don't care what kind of zip they put on the throw as long as it's a quick release. If the throw is down to second quick enough, you can bet that the shortstop has time to swoop back and make the tag on the runner.

The quick release has made basestealing a much tougher art to master. You don't see guys swiping 100 bags anymore. Sound basestealing mechanics are very important in this era of the quick release, a technique that's trick-led down to college and high school baseball.

Pitchers' use of the slide-step has also cut down on stolen base totals, but it has one big drawback: The slide-step works to the advantage of the hitter. If a pitcher slide-steps, well, chances are he's not going to throw a breaking ball. He thinks the runner has the green light so he'll avoid a pitch—the curve, for instance—that gives the runner more time to steal.

The hitter, therefore, is looking for cheese. When you see a guy moving quick like that—hey, you're going to get some cheese. And a hitter can time the fastball just right. Many guys won't throw the slide-step pitch for a strike—with the Giant pitching staff it's usually an outside fastball.

The Strategy of the Steal: an intelligent basestealer has to pick the ideal situation for a stolen base. Don't steal to pad your stats! I bat third, and as the number three hitter I'm always going to have a big bopper batting behind me, a guy who can hit home runs. I don't want to take the bat out of his hands with a caught steal—I've got to be selective.

A few guidelines on when and when not to steal: generally, don't run when the batter is behind in the count because it's easy to pitch out. A ball doesn't cost the pitcher anything in that situation. I like to run on a 1–0 pitch. But I'll also steal on the first pitch. The first pitch is often the best one to go on, especially in my spot with a power guy like Fred McGriff hitting behind me. The pitcher doesn't want to throw Fred a fastball right down Broadway and give him a chance to smash a home run. So he'll start Fred off with a changeup or a breaking ball, and that means I have more time to steal.

It all depends on the situation. In some instances I don't want to run on the first pitch. I want the pitcher to think I'm just hanging out, giving my cleanup hitter a chance to get some hacks.

A good strategy of deception, but this type of attitude can work against you. With Jack Clark hitting behind me in 1990, there were a few instances where I'd be all set to steal—I had a comfortable lead—and then I changed my mind. I didn't want to take the bat out of Jack's hands.

You can't be racked with fear as a basestealer. You have to say, "I'm going to steal this base—just try to throw me out!" Don't make excuses. It's like riding a bicycle. You have to keep getting back on until you get it right.

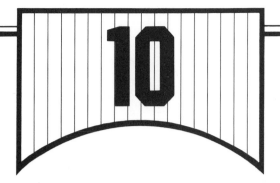

IN SEARCH OF THE GOLDEN GLOVE

FEELING comfortable is the key to success in any sport. If you try to play the outfield with an uncomfortable glove, usually you're going to have problems.

The comfort factor will dictate the ideal size of your glove: large or small, roomy pockets or small pockets, closed webbed versus open webbed—you name it.

Don't fret over choosing a glove. Just pick one that will let you get the job done. The specific model is up to you.

I've relied on the same glove—the Rawlings Pro H—since Little League. The Pro H is considered a big glove. A bigger glove comes into play on ground balls; there's enough room to give you some margin for error if you make a mistake. With a smaller glove, though, you must be more precise.

Unfortunately, my big glove came under fire prior to the 1990 season. The rule was changed to limit glove size to 13 inches; the old Rawlings I'd worn my whole life was 13¾ inches. I had to switch to a new, smaller version of the same glove.

A three-quarter-inch difference doesn't sound like much of a change, but all of a sudden the ball in the gap that used to hit the end of my glove

Find a glove that's comfortable for you and stick with it. I've used the Rawlings Pro H since Little League.

was whizzing by me on its way to the fence.

Early in spring training, after the lockout of 1990 finally ended, I started taking fly balls every day. Well, I almost dropped a lot of them because I was accustomed to catching the ball in the pocket. And with the new glove my pocket is about three-eighths of an inch smaller—not only in length, but in diameter too.

So when the ball landed in the pocket and I'd close the glove, the ball would pop back out. I had to get my other hand over there in a hurry to assist in making the catch. At the beginning of the year I caught a lot of balls with two hands. I generally favor a two-handed catch anyway, but now I was using my other hand to keep the ball in the glove.

After a month or so I adjusted; it became automatic. In spring training I was thinking about the glove too much; "God, I don't want to drop a ball out here." I got past the point of worrying and became confident I'd make the catch.

That's what you want—a glove so comfortable that you don't have to worry every time the ball is hit your way.

Caring for Your Glove

Rawlings gloves are notorious for being stiff when you buy them. It takes two weeks just to break them in. Don't try to break in a glove during the game. I'd rather break it in during batting practice, playing catch or shagging fly balls. Never play a game with a new glove that's not comfortable.

Breaking in the Glove: I stick two balls in the pocket, use adhesive tape to close it shut, and then dip the palm part of the glove and the bottom of the pocket into a whirlpool. I let it sit for about 30 seconds. Then I stick a hanger in the glove and allow it to hang-dry for two days.

After two days, when you remove the tape and take the balls out, the pocket is formed. All you have to do

is start playing catch and taking fly balls. About a week later you can use it in a game. This process works fine—the Padres' trainer taught me how to do this three years ago and the results have been excellent.

The one problem is that when you dip the glove in the water, it has a tendency to get very flimsy. Usually, if you break it in the old-fashioned way, the glove will last four or five years. But with this method—at least at the major league level—it will last only 2 to 2½ years.

Once a glove becomes flimsy I start having problems. For my style of outfield play a stiff glove is essential. The flimsier the glove, the easier it is to make a mistake.

In BP I'll occasionally use a flimsy glove to field grounders and fly balls. When you charge a base hit with a flimsy glove it will go in the pocket, but then as you start to bring the glove up, the ball will flip right out.

I want to be confident that when I close my glove around a baseball it will stay in the pocket, not pop out and start rolling away from me. With a stiff glove I know that when I reach in the pocket to grab the ball it will always be in the same spot. By the time a glove is flimsy, though, there's no precise pocket; the ball could be anywhere!

Don't waste time looking for the ball. As an outfielder you need to catch the ball cleanly and get off your throw as quickly and accurately as possible. And the right glove will allow you to do just that.

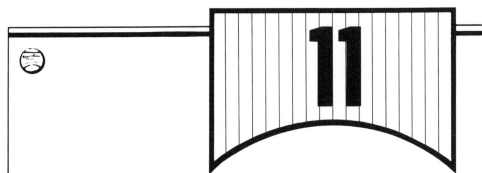

PRACTICE MAKES PERFECT

IN my earliest days as an outfielder my main concern was escaping an inning without making any mistakes. Catch the ball and throw it back to the infield as quickly as possible—I knew I didn't have the arm strength. I just wanted to get to the ball and hit my cut-off man. That was it.

When you become a professional ballplayer, though, you discover that people will exploit your weaknesses. During my first year at Walla Walla everybody was running on my arm. Everybody would grab the extra base because they knew I couldn't throw them out. Hey, even I knew I couldn't throw them out.

At the end of that first year in pro ball I finally had a winter to devote strictly to baseball—I'd always played basketball in the off-season. I made a commitment to do whatever was needed to become a better defensive player. I'd never had any problems with my hitting, but my fielding had to improve or I wouldn't make it to the big leagues.

I basically went back to school that winter and learned how to throw. I started playing long toss every day, working on refining my mechanics. And I continually searched for new ways to improve my fielding. I knew there was more to being a good outfielder than just having superior arm strength.

The next spring I met up with Tom House—at the time a Padre minor league instructor and currently the pitching coach of the Texas Rangers—and in three minutes he taught me the correct mechanics of throwing a baseball, what is known as the Captain's Wheel.

The motion is so simple; it's as if you're a captain steering the wheel of his boat. When your throwing side goes back, the other side of your body goes up. And when you throw, you pull the nonthrowing side down and the throwing side comes right over the top. You want to throw right over the top with an across-the-seams grip on the ball.

When I used to throw in high school and college, I would open up my front side. Now I come over the top and pull the nonthrowing side down as I go. If you open up you'll never get any zip on the ball. By keeping my front side closed (pulling the nonthrowing side down), I can really get some carry on my throw. Momentum is helping the ball along. Plus I'll get the rotation needed to propel the ball to its target.

You don't want to open up—which simply means your frontside shoulder stays down (instead of coming up) when you pull your throwing side back. It's impossible to generate any arm speed or momentum from this position; consequently, you won't be able to throw the ball as far.

Watch Andre Dawson during infield practice before a game. He takes a little

The Captain's Wheel: bring your throwing side back, and pull your front side down when you throw. Throw right over the top, not from a ¾ or sidearm position.

longer to release his throw, but the zip he puts on the ball—via the momentum from the Captain's Wheel—is unbelievable. He snaps that front arm up; his throwing side goes back; and momentum drives the frontside down as the throwing arm comes over the top. Dawson has the best arm of any right fielder in the game today.

The Captain's Wheel technique helped my throwing improve dramatically. The mechanics of throwing, especially if you're an outfielder, are so important. It's a long heave from way out there. A solid throw with sound mechanics should give you a legitimate crack at nailing the runner; bad mechanics will mess up your chances every time.

The best way to improve your mechanics while also increasing arm strength is the long-toss drill. Begin by throwing the ball back and forth with your teammate—perhaps 10 or 15 yards apart. Slowly increase the distance to stretch out your arm. Go as far back as you can until you start bouncing your throws. Don't worry about the height of the throw. Concentrate on rehearsing correct mechanics—the Captain's Wheel technique I talked about earlier.

Practice the long-toss drill, both in the off-season and during the season. I think it's particularly important during the season. Let's say you're having one of those games where no one hits the ball to you all day. Your only throws are to teammates in the outfield between innings. That's not enough of a workout for your throwing arm. You

Field a grounder on one knee if you have time.

need that extra throwing before the game.

Mechanics are equally important for fielding outfield grounders, those one- or two-hop base hits. You'll come across two kinds of ground balls in the outfield:

1) A ground ball that allows you enough time to get your body in front of the ball and field it cleanly (feel free to drop down on one knee). Your job is to field the ball and get it back in to the infield as quick as you can. So on a one- or two-hop base hit you don't

Charge a grounder if a runner is trying to advance a base or score. Field the ball just outside your front foot and throw it quickly.

have to charge the ball really hard. Just drop to one knee, field the ball and make a strong, accurate throw.

2) The do or die play! You know that the only way to throw the guy out is to charge the ball as hard as possible. You can't hang back and wait for the ball. As a lefty, I want to field the ball on the outside of my right foot (it's just the opposite for a righty), with my glove out in front of my foot so I can take 2½ steps and throw. The idea is to field the ball and get rid of it. If you can do it in two steps, fine. A step and

Correct throwing grip, across the seams.

a half is even better. You don't have any time to waste.

Field the ball cleanly. Get rid of it quickly. Make your throw as accurate as possible. Those are three objectives when you charge a ball. If you have great arm strength and can throw the ball on a line, hey, that's even better. Just follow the same instructions and throw the ball on a line. But if you're like me—I don't have great arm strength—you have to field the ball and get rid of it right away.

A quick release will help you as an outfielder, especially if you're not blessed with a strong arm. If my throw is right around the bag I've got a shot at nailing the runner. It's the same mentality as a catcher—he knows that a quick, accurate throw is going to do the job.

I guarantee you that every assist I

Incorrect grip, fingers placed along the seams. This will cause your throw to sail away from your intended receiver.

record is due to a quick release and accuracy. It's certainly not because of my arm strength. At Jack Murphy Stadium there's a little corner in the outfield where the ball just pops out at you—I'm there to field it, fire my throw to second, and Tony Fernandez puts his glove down and the runner slides right into the tag. I've practiced this play for seven years and it works as long as the throw is on the money.

Accuracy is the name of the game. But you can't make an accurate throw without a correct grip on the baseball. I use an across-the-seams grip on the ball. Just let it go; the ball takes a backwards spin, and when it hits the ground it will pop up and take a long, straight hop. If you throw the ball with your fingers placed along the seams, though, it's going to be angling away from the intended receiver.

Early in my career at Walla Walla I didn't even know I was supposed to grip the ball across the seams. But someone in the Padre organization knew I was messing up because Tom House came to me the first day of spring training in 1982 to straighten out my throwing. Ever since that day I've been a much better defensive player.

All outfielders dream of the perfect throw—a bullet to the third baseman from the right field corner. But what's wrong with doing the same thing—making a perfect throw—but getting it there in a hop or two? If you release it quickly enough there is nothing wrong with a two-hop throw to the bag that nails the runner.

Here is my favorite drill for accuracy: Take a bag of balls out with you to right field. (Center fielders and left fielders can practice this drill from their respective positions.) Remove the balls from the bag and place them—one at a time—in the position they'd be in if you were charging a ball hit to you in right. Pick the ball up in your glove, take your two steps to get set and try to make an accurate one-hop throw to third. Do this over and over and over again. It's the best way I know of to develop accuracy.

Do not allow for anything more than a two-hop throw to third. More than two hops will defeat the purpose. The first hop is the long hop. The second hop is the short hop. If it bounces a third time you've got no chance.

Always throw across the seams. Take one or two steps and get off a perfect one- or two-hop throw to third.

After you toss a bag's worth of balls—about 30—to third, it's time to make 30 throws to home plate. Same thing; get the ball there accurately on only one or two hops.

This drill helps you not only with accuracy, but with your mechanics as well. Charge, close it up, over the top and one or two hops to the target. I practiced this drill four years in a row during the off-season, three times per week. It's 30 throws to third base; 30 throws to home; 60 throws in total, three days per week.

Get to the point where you can do this at full speed. Gradually, you'll start to see some improvement. You'll say, "Hey, I'm getting pretty accurate with that throw."

Accuracy is the determining factor on many close plays. A long throw from the right field corner had better be on target or you can forget about recording the out. Don't count on an infielder bailing you out by diving for an errant throw, whirling back to the bag and making the tag.

Rob Picciolo, a coach with the Padres, hits me fly balls on a regular basis. Rob rips a few balls down the line, I'll go get it, turn and throw the ball on a fly to second—boom, all the second baseman has to do is apply the tag. That's a play I can handle. But the throws to third and home require constant repetition.

Darren Jackson, the Padre center fielder, and I have our own little battle during infield practice prior to the game: We're looking to see who can catch it, get rid of it and be accurate—

forget arm strength, just put it right on the bag so the infielder doesn't have to move. The third baseman stands right behind the bag and if he has to move his feet, then the throw is not accurate.

I know that all my hard work at mastering those two throws—to third and to home—has paid off. I'm right around the bag. It's almost like a pitcher knowing he can put the ball wherever he wants. I'm confident my throw is going to be on target.

Hitting the cut-off man is equally important. It's an easy art to perfect—with practice, of course. Grab a bag of balls and head out to the fence or wall of your local stadium. Ask one of your teammates to assume a cut-off position and practice hitting him with an accurate throw. Two rules apply to cut-off plays:

Rule #1: If a ball is still rolling around after it hits the wall, pick it up with your glove hand.

Rule #2: If a ball has stopped rolling, then you can barehand it cleanly before making your throw.

In either case, you don't have the luxury of taking four or five steps before releasing the throw. Get the ball and send it to the cut-off man. Put all the responsibility on his shoulders.

A typical cut-off situation: A base hit with a slow runner on second. You realize he's not going home; instead of charging it hard, then, you field the ball from your normal position and try to hit the cut-off man—the infielder who is standing there with his hands in the air.

The goal is to hit the cut-off man somewhere between his elbows and his belt. He should have no trouble catching the ball if your throw hits its mark.

So just grab a bag of balls, head to the fence and repeat each phase of the cut-off play—turn, pick up the ball, hit your cut-off man—repeat until the bag is empty.

If the baserunner is on his way to third or home, the infielder (your cut-off man) will be standing on the infield between his bag and home plate. Try to hit the cut-off man on a line. If you can't hit him on a line, then release the ball quickly enough to give him enough time to complete the relay.

Proper footwork—the ability to get into position to make an accurate throw—is another crucial skill. My basic theory is that you run as hard as possible when you're charging a ball. A few steps before grabbing it, though, you gather your forces to control momentum. This is tough to do on artificial turf, as the ball is bearing down on you in a hurry. On grass, however, charge until you're a couple of steps from the ball, gather yourself, field the ball, get rid of it and be accurate.

Forget about throwing guys out if your feet get all tangled up at the point of release. Assists will come to you if your footwork, arm strength and mechanics are in synch.

Only in 1986 did I compile an outrageous assist total—I threw out 19 or 20 guys. Runners kept testing me and I kept throwing them out. I won my first Gold Glove Award that year and all of a sudden I had a reputation as a great fielder—"He's a Gold Glove winner; don't run on him!"

I haven't had more than 13 assists since then, but people around baseball respect me because they know I work hard at my fielding. I'm out there every day taking fly balls, working on charging the ball and getting a good jump. The hard work has paid off!

Getting a good jump on the ball does depend to some extent on instinct, no question. It requires a special talent to see a ball hit the bat and know immediately where you have to go.

Eyesight plays an integral part in sound defense. But sometimes your eyes can fool you. You need something else to guide you to the ball. You see a guy take a big hack and you think, "He really got that one!" But your ears may tell you another story.

Playing defense is based on a combination of sights, sounds and instincts. The crack of the bat. The trajectory of the ball in flight. The reaction of the hitter after he completes his swing. Watch everything carefully. Listen to the sound of the ball hitting the bat.

Eyesight is the most important factor in getting a good jump on the ball. What you see is usually what's happening, but there are exceptions to every rule.

We have a lot of big, strong hitters in the National League. Kevin Mitchell, formerly of the San Francisco Giants and now with the Seattle Mariners, can smack a home run with only one hand. He hit a ball at Jack Murphy Stadium last year that was unbelievable: from

The drop-step and cross over: If the ball's hit over your left shoulder, take a step back with your left foot and cross your right foot over. *Don't* backpedal; see how I'm ready to angle backward.

my perspective in right field it looked as if I should break in on the ball. The crack of the bat also told me to break in. But my brain told me to break back—this is a strong guy we're talking about! I broke back, ran to the wall and leaped up to make the catch.

The moral of this story is trust your eyes and ears, but also remember to learn as much as you can about the opposing hitters. Mitchell is one of the strongest guys I've ever seen in the big leagues—he can hit a ball with one hand, perched on one foot, and still hit it over the fence. Since I was prepared for Mitchell—since I knew what he was capable of doing—I was able to go back for the ball and bring it down.

Here's what you do when the ball is hit over your head: Begin with a drop-step; if it's hit over my left shoulder, for instance, I want to step back with my left foot, then cross over my right leg—and keep crossing over—until I reach the ball. Don't backpedal to make the catch. We call that drifting. It's a great way to get hurt and a poor way to try to catch the ball.

So if the ball is hit over the left shoulder, simply drop-step with your left foot and then cross over. If it's hit over the right shoulder, just drop-step with your right foot and then cross over. The drop-step and cross over are the first order of business on any ball hit over your head.

Contrary to what you might think, it's also okay to take a drop-step back on a little blooper hit in front of you. Drop-step and come in to make the catch. It's easier to break in for a ball

If the ball's hit over your right shoulder, drop your right foot back and cross over with your left.

than to race back. Never break in on a ball hit over your head.

When a ball is hit over your head you're not really running; you're cross-over. Occasionally you might turn and sprint, but we'll get to that a little later.

Young outfielders tend to backpedal,

sort of a drifting-into-outer-space type of motion. How many times have you seen a Little League game where a kid drifts back until he falls over and hits his head on the ground? The ball's rolling around out there and the guy who hit the ball is circling the bases. So I try to emphasize the drop-step, though it does take awhile to click.

Most Little League coaches try to hide their worst defensive players in the outfield, particularly right field. A kid who doesn't have the confidence of his coach isn't going to be comfortable. But judging a fly ball isn't as easy as it looks. It's tough for adults too.

The Pop Fly Payoff on Sundays at "The Murph" (Jack Murphy Stadium) is a good example—most of the contestants just can't catch them. It's not the easiest skill to master. Like anything else it requires patience and practice.

With experience, you'll learn to apply the different aspects of fielding we've discussed—a quick release, the Captain's Wheel, an across-the-seams grip, the drop-step and cross over, getting a good jump on the ball—and gradually you'll become a better outfielder.

One of the hardest things to grasp about playing the outfield is that it's okay to take your eyes off the ball to get into a better position to make the catch. You're running to an imaginary spot—the point in the outfield where you can catch the ball.

Right as the ball is hit you realize you can't make the catch simply by watching the flight of the ball. So you sprint as hard as you can for five steps, turn around, and try to locate the ball. If you still can't reach it, put your head down and drive a couple more steps until you can pick up the ball and make the grab.

Sooner or later you're going to realize you can either make the catch or you can't. And if you can't catch the ball, you want to rush to a position—usually playing the carom off the wall—where you can get the ball back in and hold the guy to a double.

But as I drive those five steps and look up for the ball for the first time I'm faced with a big decision: do I put my head down again and run, or can I make the catch while following the flight of the ball? Seeing the ball is better. You don't want to bust back until the last second and then fling your glove in the air, hoping the ball drops right in.

If a ball is hit really well—all the way back to the wall—you might take 10 steps before looking up to locate it in flight. This is a skill that comes with experience!

Chili Davis, back in '84 or '85 with the Giants, hit a line drive that I thought was heading for the wall. I was playing him in shallow right field. I turned and sprinted back to play the ball off the wall and glanced up to realize, "Oh, man, I can catch this thing!" I jumped up and snagged the ball.

All the people watching me must have thought it was a heck of a catch. But in my mind I never thought I could make the play. I thought I was going

The cross over in action: proper footwork for catching a fly ball.

back to time the carom and all of a sudden the ball's in my glove.

Fulton County Stadium (Atlanta) and Busch Stadium (St. Louis) have huge gaps in the outfield, power alleys that seem to go on forever. I do a lot of running in those parks. At Jack Murphy, though, I can only run so far before I have to look—the wall comes up on me quickly.

But in St. Louis I can just run endlessly. George Hendrick once hit a ball to me in right-center and to this day I don't know how I caught it.

In St. Louis they tell you to give them the lines and take away the gaps. I'm playing close to right-center and Hendrick smokes a ball into the gap—it's like Death Valley out there. I ran a few steps, knew I couldn't catch it. I ran a bit more, looked up and realized I still didn't have a chance. Then I ran some more and there it was—I leaped from a dead run, put my glove up and—boom—the ball went right in.

My first reaction was, "Ah, I caught it." It takes awhile to gear down. You can't just stop on a dime. I ran into the wall, flicked the ball back in and just enjoyed the feeling of satisfaction.

Now, I don't know how to dive for a baseball. I will slide for a ball or fall forward to catch it, but I really don't know how to dive. I'm not an Andy Van Slyke, who can flat-out lie there and make the play. It's an instinctive reaction.

I do the next best thing, which is to slide; I can keep the ball in front of me if I miss it. If you dive and miss there's nothing you can do to stop the ball from continuing on its way.

Van Slyke is not only a great diver, but a natural outfielder—he can play all three outfield posts with authority. He's settled on center as his best position; center field is by far the hardest of the three to master.

All three outfield positions have their advantages and disadvantages. As a center fielder, for instance, you can see what the pitcher is going to throw and where he's trying to put the ball. You correlate that information with what type of hitter you have at the plate and position yourself accordingly. But because you have so much ground to cover it's still a tough job.

I prefer either left or right. The toughest part of playing the corners is adjusting for the angle: Balls hit to right field off the bat of a righthander will generally slice, while lefthanders will hook the ball to right; in left field it's just the opposite, lefthanders slice the ball and righthanders hook the ball.

Say I'm in right field and a right-hander hits the ball to right-center. That's not a tough play because I know the ball is going to slice back towards me as I'm going after it. A lefthanded hitter hooking the ball down the line in right is a different story. The ball is moving away from me, making it harder to cut it off and get it back to the infield.

I consider myself a corner person. My lack of arm strength makes it hard for me to play center; even if I charge the ball hard I still have a long throw to the plate. And I've got the mound to contend with too. On the corners there are no obstacles. You can use the grass to get that long hop you need to reach first or third base.

So I'm comfortable in left or right. I can play center, but that's not using my skills to the best advantage. I can go get it, hit my cut-off man—no problem. The long throw from deep center to home plate is the one I can't make.

Remember, then, that you need more than good speed to play center; you need excellent arm strength. I feel comfortable sprinting to left-center or right-center to field a ball. Even a ball hit straight over my head is no trouble. I know I have more room than in any other part of the park to go get it. But the throw is just so long that it requires tremendous arm strength to heave the ball to the plate.

A lot of the top right fielders in the National League have great arm strength, but how many guys can put the whole package together?

Andre Dawson has a great arm. His accuracy is good. But he doesn't get rid of the ball quickly enough. Darryl Strawberry has a great arm. His accuracy is suspect. And he doesn't get rid of it quickly enough. Glenn Wilson had a great arm. He got rid of the ball quickly. But he had no accuracy. And as far as Tony Gwynn is concerned: I get rid of it in a hurry. I'm accurate. But I don't have good arm strength.

None of the best right fielders have all the qualities you look for in a top defensive player. We're out there using our positives to outweigh our negatives. The question isn't how many qualities you lack but, instead, how hard are you willing to work to improve the qualities you do have?

I'm one of those guys who has to work hard to hide what I don't do well. Not just hide the problems, but strive to overcome them. I've tried to improve my arm strength, and I hope that all my hard work will pay off. If guys try to run on me they're going to be thrown out—that's how confident I feel right now.

Baseball has a tendency to be one-sided; everybody focuses on the offensive end of the game. But in the National League you're a much more valuable player if you can do both. If you can hit and field you're a double threat. People will be more likely to give you an opportunity to play.

The Gold Glove—as far as I'm concerned—is the ultimate individual award in baseball. Winning it, for me, was the greatest because no one thought I could do it. And I've done it five times. For a guy who wasn't supposed to be able to play defense, it feels pretty good.

The Gold Glove is even more gratifying than winning four batting titles. People knew I could hit, but defensively no one gave me a chance. I still may not be as good as some right fielders in the game, but I do what's necessary to be successful. Fielding is not a God-given talent. I've had to work hard for what I've achieved. I want you to do the same.

INDEX

Index

ABOUT THE AUTHORS

Jim Rosenthal is Executive Editor at Weider Health & Fitness, where he is responsible for editing, assigning and writing articles on weight training, diet, aerobic exercise, and other health issues. He is also sports editor of *Men's Fitness* magazine. With Nolan Ryan and Tom House he coauthored *Nolan Ryan's Pitcher's Bible*, an instructional book. A native of New York City, he lives with his family in Santa Monica, California.

Tony Gwynn is the rightfielder for the San Diego Padres. He holds four National League batting titles (1984, 1987, 1988, 1989), and through 1991 his lifetime average is .328. A seven-time All Star, Tony has also won five Gold Gloves for his excellence in the field. He is a founding partner of the San Diego School of Baseball, and has been active in the Just Say No Foundation, the Hire-a-Youth program in San Diego County, and as a volunteer with San Diego's Casa de Amparo (House of Refuge), which provides shelter and counseling for young victims of abuse. A native of Los Angeles, Gwynn and his family now live in San Diego, California.